Intervenor Funding for Public Participation
in Federal Environmental Decision-making:
A Short History

By David McRobert
Fellow, Faculty of Env. Studies
York University

April 1987

Contents

Introduction: Revisiting a "Hard Choice"

Democratic Theory and the Modern State

Policy Responses to Demands for Participation

Public Participation in Environmental Decision-Making

The Need for Intervenor Funding

The Berger Inquiry: A Breakthrough

The Federal Response in Canada

Reaction, Retrenchment and NIMBY

Mechanisms for Intervenor Funding

      1). Approaches to Funding

      2). A Modest Proposal for Funding Criteria

Conclusion: The Legacy of the Berger Inquiry

Notes

Introduction: Revisiting a "Hard Choice"

The publication of a new biography on Thomas Berger (1) has once again rekindled an interest in a famous episode in Canadian political economy, the Mackenzie Valley Pipeline Inquiry (2). While the Inquiry was important in many respects, it is interesting to note that Berger, who was appointed as Commissioner for the Inquiry (which explains why it subsequently became known as "the Berger Inquiry") by Liberal Cabinet in 1974, considers widespread public support for intervenor funding as its most important accomplishment. (3)

This tells us something about Berger's understanding of natural justice and fairness. Arguably, Berger felt that commissions of inquiry could have an important impact on public policy. He admired the work that had been done by other judges such as Emmett Hall. In the 1960s, while a Justice of Supreme Court of Canada, Hall had headed up an important inquiry on health care in Canada. This inquiry had eventually led to some important reforms in the Canadian health care system.

Berger had also been impressed by numerous other innovative royal commissions, as Page (3a) argues. In devising a satisfactory process to guage public opinion on the massive pipeline contemplated by the federal government and industry, Berger took the view that emerging principles of administrative law must be reflected the structure of the Inquiry.(3b) As a result, intervenor funding was provided to many public interest and native groups to encourage participation.

Since the Berger Inquiry, intervenor funding has become a growth industry in Canada, especially in relation to the fight for aboriginal rights by Indian and Inuit groups. This has led some critics to pose questions about its efficacy. Indeed, some have argued that native groups should not be funded to publicly embarass officials and lobby overseas. (4) While these arguments do not appear to have influenced policy-making on intervenor funding to date, it remains to be seen what the eventual outcome of this pattern of discontent will be over the long term.

The history of the growth of demand for increased public involvement in government decision-making is long and complicated and few have provided an accurate survey of the key factors that led up to the break-throughs that have taken place in Canada and elsewhere. As the discussion below will demonstrate, the environmental movement provided a strong impetus for greater participation in environmental decision-making in the United States and Canada, and later in Europe and other industrialised nations. A widespread perception had developed that the quality of decisions made by leaders had to be improved and brought into line with public concerns that "the environment was being destroyed." In part, this perception had been spurred by the spread of pollutants such as DDT and the over whelming growth of raw material consumption in the industrialized West.

Public participation (5) was conceived as a means to assauge citizens who wanted these matters dealt with and simultaneously allow them to vent their anger to officials. The basic rationale for public participation was that the quality of decision-making could be improved through productive use of inputs and perceptions from private citizens and public interest groups. If increased participation in decision-making is accepted as a public good, it stands to reason that intevenor funding is an important adjunct measure in support of groups and individuals who choose to particpate.

As we will see below, experience in Canada suggests that public participation became a popular approach for debating many resource development and planning issues in the 1970s. In part, this contribution was enhanced by funding intervenor groups who have become a type of watchdog. However, after a decade of wrangling and experimentation many governments and federal agencies in Canada still are reluctant to support public interest groups with funding and technical support. Moreover, the courts in Canada have also limited the legitimacy and importance of public interest interventions in regulatory decision-making. In recent decisions they have upheld decisions made by agencies not to award costs to intervenor groups that have contributed significantly to policy-making through participation in regulatory hearings despite express provisions in enabling legislation giving these bodies the power to do so. (8)

This trend suggests a backlash may be developing in Canada towards public interest interventions in policy-making. Thus, it is indeed feasible that after a few decades of progressive reform in the area of public participation and intervenor funding, Canada may have begun to move towards the position followed in other common law jurisdictions, particularly the United States where enthusiasm for participation has never been as great. (6)

Against this backdrop are other signs that intervenor funding for public interest interventions has become an important element in the Canadian polity. It could be argued that in an era when the Charter of Rights and Freedoms promises to revamp the structure and function of many government agencies, the importance of this reform must be safeguarded from political interference. Public interest interventions help to ensure that the decisions ultimately taken by government reflect concerns expressed by public interest groups about the need for justice and equity in decision-making. For example, the Ontario Cabinet recently decided to force the Ontario Municipal Board to exercize its discretion with respect to awards for costs to a public interest group fighting to preserve agricultural land. (7) In doing so, they confirmed that intergenerational equity issues such as the future scarcity of farmland in Canada do have a place in regulatory decision-making.

In this paper, the arguments in support of intervenor funding for environmental decision-making will be reviewed in the context of broadening public participation in government regulation of the environment and environmental assessment. Literature in field will be reviewed (9) but the analysis is primarily historical.

The first sections of the paper survey the factors which contributed to widespread support for greater public participation in developed nations. In addition, some of the arguments for funding will be reviewed in leading up to an examination of the Berger Inquiry.

In the subsequent sections, the role of the Berger Inquiry in transforming public attitudes towards participation will be considered. Most of the analysis will focus on the development of intervenor funding for the federal Environmental Assessment and Review Process (EARP). However, attention will also be directed towards practices of provincial governments in Canada and patterns of support in other common law jurisdictions.

The intent of the paper will be to bring to bear a critical analysis on the issues related to public participation and intervenor funding and suggest proposals for reform. In the course of our journey, we will dip into many areas of law and public policy related to democratic theory, administration and social justice. It is on the first of these subjects that our journey must begin.

Democratic Theory and the Modern State

Prior to setting out the arguments for public participation and intervenor funding, it is necessary to review the factors that contributed to widespread demands for change in the dominant decision-making practices of large government agencies in the 1960s and 1970s. These demands were largely attributable to a perception that had emerged that government had become too large and bureaucratic and was insensitive to the needs of the public. In the process, elements of responsibility and legitimacy had become muddled and many people felt alienated by the impersonal nature of the modern technocratic state. (10)

In the eyes of these alienated people, the emergence of the modern technocratic state seemed almost inexplicable. The irony of this observation is that the foundation of the modern technocratic state is representative democracy. This foundation reflects, in turn, the legacies of John Locke, Jeremy Bentham, James Mill, Jean Jacques Rousseau, John Stuart Mill and G.D.H. Cole. These thinkers encouraged the development of a political tradition in the West which held that "men" should participate actively in the institutions of government as a natural right. (11)

In small-scale agricultural communities, such a model of participation may have been feasible and could even have provided a measure of participatory democracy. (12) However, with the emergence of industrialism as the dominant mode of production and ideological framework in the eighteenth century, and the shift from status to contract as a basis for social interaction in growing communities, participation was deemphasized. (13) The need for alternative centralized administrative agencies to displace the role of the local Justices of the Peace and the Gentry (14) in England became evident, as Arthurs (15) has argued in his recent treatise, Without the Law. This process initiated a movement that continued to accelerate through the 19th century and culminated in the emergence of modern industrial society. In this configuration of the state, opportunities to participate are constrained by the complexity of decisions that must be made, as well as a host of other factors. (16)

For decades in this century, conventional wisdom held that public paricipation was not feasible for reasons of practicality and efficiency and that the masses were not interested in particpating anyway. As Pateman argues, a review of the findings of twentieth century political sociologists reveals that "the outstanding characteristic of most citizens, more especially those in the lower socio-economic status groups, is a general lack of interest in politics and political activity...." (17) This literature attributes this lack of interest to authoritarian and non-participatory attitudes pervasive in the lower socio-economic groups and holds that that mass participation from this group is unlikely and perhaps even inappropriate.

Foremost among the political sociologists who rejected earlier democratic theories and notions of participatory democracy was Joseph Schumpeter. In his classic text, Capitalism, Socialism and Democracy (18), Schumpeter argues that British liberal thinkers presumed that universal application of the ideal of democratic participation was appropriate. However this is not a realistic presumption because it is predicated on attitudes that were not borne out by experience:

> if the opinions and desires of individual citizens were perfectly definite and independent data for the democratic process to work with, and if everyone acted on them with ideal rationality and prompitude, it would not necessarily follow that the political decisons produced by that process from the raw material of those individual positions would represent anything that could in any convincing sense be called the will of the people. It is not only inconceivable but, whenever individual wills are much divided, very likely that the political decisions produced will not conform to "what people want." (19)

To summarize the views of Schumpeter and other political sociologists, the classical view of democratic man is hopelessly unrealistic. The facts of political life do not suggest a widespread desire to participate in decision-making. (20) Moreover, a movement towards widespread participation could upset the stability of democratic political systems.

Coupled with the growth of a scientific establishment in government and the logic of Schumpeter and his cohorts was a movement towards elite participation as a surrogate for wide public involvement in decision-making. According to this approach, relevant information about a major project or policy which might affect a local population could be provided to an elite of educated or politically-active members in the community. (21) In the process a large body of the public was not fully informed about risks that were being taken by policy-makers or gaps in knowledge that existed. From this perspective it is easier to understand why nuclear power was seen as a great technological achievement in the early 1960s. Not a word about potential environmental impacts was uttered until much later, when the possible consequences of radioactive contamination and the difficlties with waste disposal became more widely known.

The bureaucratization of many spheres of public life in the eary 20th century had a stifling impact on individuals interested in challenging the dominant views of government and industry. As Alford argues, the proliferation of specialized agencies designed to deal with increased volumes of individuals making greater demands on government stimulated a growth of interest in the policy-making mechanisms of government, especially the regulatory spheres. (22) This became clear, for example, in the area of consumer protection law where considerable public distrust of both government and industry had been spurred by the activism of "Nader's Raiders" and their Canadian counterparts. (23)

These factors alone do not explain the growth in demands for participation in public decision-making that took place in the 1960s. To understand this we also must consider other factors. Wilkinson argues that the desire among many urban North Americans to participate in decision-making may be explained in terms of the following factors:

> rising levels of education; increasing size, complexity and pervasiveness of organizations; the "narrow rationality" of institutional decision-making; questioning the effectiveness of voting and representation; major cultural shift, and response to government. (24)

Another factor which contributed to the demnds for public participation was a rather sudden drop in opinions about the value of scientific research and the authority of scientists. (25) This may be related to the emergence of the counter-culture movement as a political element and the horror of this counter-culture in considering the role of the military-industrial complex that had perpetuated a bizzare war in Vietnam. (26) However, numerous events took place in the 1960s which fueled this distrust in the capacity of engineers and scientists. Two examples are the Torry Canyon Oil spill and the Minamato mercury poisoning problems in Japan.

A fourth factor that explains the increased demand for participation was an implicit critique of consumerism. (27) Industrial nations had experienced a tremendous increase in prosperity in the 1960s and early 1970s. Cheap fuel and population growth had spurred remarkable urban expansion. As a result, the scale and potential impact of development projects increased dramatically. (28) Massive energy and transportation proposals (which became known as "megaprojects") were contemplated by urban-industrial planners. While the potential for benefit in the urban centres was great, many people perceived that these projects could cause severe environmental disruption in the hinterland. (29) These perceptions were fostered by famous pollution cases like KVP (30) and the contamination of waters fished by the Ojibwa of Grassy Narrows with mercury. (31)

International experience with public participation was also beginning to attract attention and providing support for increased public involvement in decision-making. For example, in Sweden experiments with neighborhood councils and tenant organizations had proven very successful. (32) These experiments drew media coverage in North America and this, in turn, fostered a widespread perception that more could be done to democratize urban planning in Canada and the United States.

In addition to these successful international experiences, the advance of welfare services contributed to demands for increased particpation in neighborhood planning and city planning. As Janowitz (33) states

> ..with the advent of the welfare state the dimension of territoriality -- the residential community -- moves into the forefront of political rhetoric and conflict. In other words under advanced industrialism, political leaders find it necessary to augment the appeals to social class with those advocating commmunity and community "equality".

While the exact meaning of the last phrase is unclear, it is apparent a generalized perception had developed among planners that public participation was a reality of resource planning in the late 1960s and early 1970s. This led many academics to advocate forms of neighborhood government and extensive public consultation, arguing that these institutions could even apply in major urban cities. (34)

All of these factors combined in a unique way in the 1960s to challenge the dominant orthodoxy with respect to public participation in government decision-making. A new view of democratic government emerged in the process, fostered by the counter-culture movement of the Beat Generation. (35) In essence, the youth of the 1960s did not trust government and this distrust spilled over into spheres of public life and was reflected in this demand for access to decision-makers (36).

To summarize this discussion, it is appparent that argument in favour of wider public participation in regulatory and policy decision-making flowed from four key propositions:

1. Affected persons would otherwise be unable to express their views through the media or lobbying can have an input into the decision-making process;

2. Citizens and interest groups may provide important information to decision-makers, especially when the weighting process for trading-off the values involved cannot be easily quantified;

3. If the process is open to public review, the accountability and legitimacy of administrative and political decision-makers is likely to be re-inforced. An open process puts pressure on administrators to follow required procedures in all cases and allows the public to distinguish between political and administrative decisions. (37)

4. Since the public can clearly see that all issues have been fully and carefully considered in all cases, public confidence in the reviewers and decision-makers is increased and enhanced.

These arguments were invoked by many public interest groups and had an impact on the practices and procedures of many agencies and departments of government in the industrialized West. (39) However, this impact was not always favourable in terms of the desire to increase participation.

Policy Responses to Demands for Participation

The state has responded in quite different ways to demands for increased participation. In the areas of urban planning it has been difficult to deny increased public access to many of the structures and processes. (40) This undoubtedly has served to appease many people. (41) Nevertheless, it is often difficult to integrate the public into decision-making for the reasons that Schrumpeter has offered which were surveyed above. (42) Moreover, often the state is merely acting as a mediator between different groups of citizens in struggles over power and resources and one must ask whether this battle is better left to other fora. (43)

In the United States, the need for new participation structures and processeswas felt primarily in the area of water management. (44) Conflicts were emerging between different types of allocation of water resources, promoted in part by a phenomenal amount of urban growth in North America. Citizen groups that opposed the construction of large dams felt they were incredibly out-matched when it came challenging these projects and made their views known through the media. Moreover, the attempts by the U.S. Army Corps of Engineers to quell public resistance proved something of a fiasco. (45)

The problem with these proposals often stemmed from the fact that the planners and engineers involved did not delineate the people who would be impacted carefully enough, nor did they properly consider some of the negative consequences of large scale flooding of farmland and other natural areas. (46) Moreover, these planners also appeared arrogant and totally insensitive to the desires of the public to have an input in the decisions that were being taken. In the view of some citizens these planners were extremely anti-democratic, as documentation from a project in Ontario suggests. (47)

These early efforts served to bring into focus the "motivation" for these projects and raised suspicion in the minds of many that technocrats in burgeoning government agencies had to be brought under control.(48) This philosophy of public intervention was evident in Ontario when the Porter Commission on Electrical Utilities was undertaken in the late 1970s. Environmental groups raised serious questions about the need for construction of additional nuclear plants in Ontario. (49) In the process, the groups forced Ontario Hydro to back down on grand plans to build nuclear plants throughout southern Ontario and probably saved taxpayers billions of dollars in the process.

These examples show that in many cases public interest intervention would not be required if regulatory agencies were doing their jobs properly in an open and accessible fashion. As McKay notes in discussion of the Atomic Energy Control Board (AECB), some agencies often seem to deliberately mislead the public instead. For example, some of the concerns about the inadequacy of regulatory practices raised by interest groups with respect to radiation in the Port Hope area in the 1970s include the following:

1. the effectiveness of enforcement of past and present regulations;

2. the adequacy of the regulations;

3. the responsibililtiy/liability for physical and personal damage;

4 the conflicts and gaps in various jurisdictions related to regulation; and

5. access to information and secrecy in the nuclear industry. (51)

All of these concerns reflected problems in regulatory decision-making which stemmed, in part, from strong linkages between government and industry in the nuclear energy field. The fact that higher standards have now been eliminated and part of the secrecy described above has been punctured can be attributed in part to the work of groups like Energy Probe.

Arguably, the public and these groups should be permitted to participate when important decisions are made in these spheres to ensure these kinds of problems are minimized, if not eliminated entirely, in the future. However, money is needed to help such groups participate in regulatory decision-making and do original research. In this case the Port Hope citizens who brought about attention to these deficiencies were extremely motivated and willing to invest considerable amounts of time and energy to stir up controversy and prompt government action on the issue. (52) However, in the future it is essential that these groups be encouraged to contribute to hearings on standard setting and particpate in a pro-active fashion to prevent these sorts of problems from arising.

From this perspective, the issue becomes "how can one involve the public in an optimal way." Numerous frameworks have been devised to explain different types of participation in the modern industrial states. (53) These include the famous model devised by Sherry Arnstein in 1969 and modified by numerus planners and environmental scholars since that time. (54) In essence, Arnstein's model established eight tiers of citizen participation as outlined in Figure 1. Her approach has been modified by Thomsen (55) and this latter model, which is also outlined in Figure 1, will be employed here to describe different types of policy responses to demands for public participation.

According to Thomsen, four policy responses can be identified: neutral relationships, mutual accomodation, innovative conflict and disintegrative conflict. (56) In neutral relationships, non-interfererce prevails. Formal bureaucracies continue to hum along without a great deal of fuss about whether the public wants to participate in what they are doing. This approach to public participation would be reflected in the practices of agencies like the AECB. (57) Public interest groups are viewed as difficult and hyperactive children and treated in a paternalistic manner. Procedures employed by these agencies may rely on natural justice but discretion is invoked to ensure that public participation is minimized. (58)

Innovative conflict is one of the most popular approaches to public participation in environmental decision-making because interest groups usually have some degree of power. This power may include direct interventions at hearings, cross-examination of witnesses and opportunities for media exposure and confrontation of officials. As a result, groups are often able to propose alternative actions as well as oppose the option favoured by the agency.

Mutual accomodation requires a considerable expansion in public input. Conflicts are smoothed over because agencies take the views of public interest into account. The intent of the agency is to build a consensus for its plans and "stir up the pot" just enough to give the stakeholders in the process a sense that the proposed project or policy has been revamped to take their views into account. This approach may be important when government feels it must act quickly.

The last form of public participation that sometimes emerges in fairly unstructured situations is disintegrative conflict. In these cases, private forces and project proponents or decision-makers will conflict over a proposal. Often the private actors will have material well-being at stake, and will be extrememly motivated in defending their interests. This can result in frenzied ideological outbursts as the various actors in the process take "pot shots" at each other through the media or in public fora (59). Members of environmental activist groups such as Greenpeace often will employ this technique in the early stages of their lobbying efforts.

In terms of the classical model of liberal democratic society, none of these models of participation really meets a desirable standard of public involvement. Moreover, these techniques really do not address the fundamental problems with public policy-making in modern industrial capitalism. For example, marxists would criticize the attempt to "participate the public" that agencies undertake as grossly unfair and inadequate.(60) They would assert that most regulatory techniques and processes are manipulated or controlled by the industries who have "captured" the regulators. Thus, regulatory agencies fail to control industry and participation becomes a means to politically cope with public concerns while simultaneously allowing private corporations to continue to maximize short-term profits and promote economic growth by reinvesting capital into Canada. (61)

Whether or not one agrees with the marxist analysis of the problem of agency capture, the need for some kind of mechanism to appease public interest groups has become a fact of political life in most industrial nations. This has motivated some regulators to establish an oral hearing format as a technique for monitoring public concerns in many spheres of policy-making. However, this approach had a special impact in the environmental sphere and it is to an examination of this phemenona that we now must turn.

Public Participation in Environmental Decision-making

Having set out the background for the growth of public interest in participation in decision-making in a generic sense, I now wish to examine how these arguments were applied in the environmental area.

In its most elemental form the argument for public participation in environmental decision-making rests on ther premise that everyone is an expert on the environment, and as experts, they all have opinions on how to protect or develop it. (62) Moreover, public participation was seen by some officials as an option for quelling the potential for "anarchic rebellion" that they saw lurking in the protests against the Vietnam War and the lack of civil rights for blacks in the United States. (63)

There were other reasons for the demand to participate in decisions made about the environment. The experience in the Soviet Union with environmental conservation suggested the dangers of rampant technocracy. When questions about pollution of major lakes and rivers, wolf control and the damming of major rivers aros in the 1960s, the questioning individuals and groups was silenced or discredited. (64) Until recently, opportunities to participate in public review of government policy were extremely limited. Thanks to the influence of inquiries in the Canadian north, it appears that a public review was undertaken for a major plan to develop a number of northern rivers. This review scuttled the plan and appears to have brought about a major shift in Soviet attitudes on the value of participation in decision-making. (65)

Another factor that contributed to the growth of interest in public participation in environmental decision-making was the Stockholm Conference on the Human Environment sponsored by the United Nations in 1972. For two years prior to the conference, national statments had been prepared by most democratic nations.

(66) A series of public meetings were held in Canada and members of public interest groups and citizens participated in them. These meetings generated considerable interest and were widely covered by the media. In addition, they provided a model for more conferences that followed over the next fifteen years. (67)

The final factor that motivated demands for increased participation was the emergence of new private groups and public agencies whose attention focused exclusively on environmental issues. In the United States thousands of environmental groups emerged almost overnight. While proportionately fewer took root in Canada, their effectiveness in heightening public awareness of environmental matters is undeniable. The stunts of Greenpeace activists drew media attention and wide public sympathy. In turn, governments responded by creating new agencies to deal exclusively with environmental issues. (68)

In doing so they established an informal support network for the public interst groups because those hired by the government agencies had often been involved in environmental groups prior to becoming bureacrats. All of this activity served to motivate universities to develop significant innovations in curricula in order to accomodate this demand for bureaucrats and activists. (69)

With all these educated and committed people willing to take up the banner to protect the environment, it is not surprising that the demands for public participation in environmental decision-making began to reach a feverish pitch in both the

United States and Canada. The environmental movement was aided by the presence of readily identifiable spokes people in government and the media such as Barry Commoner, Rachel Carson, Ralph Nader, and Senators Kennedy and Muskie. (74) These spokespeople put pressure on the United States to respond to widespread discontent and Congress responded by passing the National Environmental Policy Act (NEPA) in 1969. (75)

The Act and provided powers to regulate pollution of air and water by industry. In addition, the NEPA embraced a practice philosophy and took an entirely new approach to environmental decision-making based on environmental impact assessment (EIA or EA). This procedure required a proponent of a major project to submit an environmental impact statement (EIS) to the EPA and make it avalable for public review. (76)

In some respects, NEPA was a breakthough (77). As discussion has already suggested in relation to water projects, public participation did not play a major role in decisiion-making in the United States. (78) As Richardson (79) shows in his review of resource decision-making in the 1950s, politicians repeatedly deflected demands for public participation. Instead there was a tendency to rely on cost-benefit analysis (CBA) as the key decision-making technique used for assesssing projects. The main objective of EIA in its infant conception was to have the public provide information that would actually be required for the final decision in a fashion analogous to CBA. (80) According to Armour, EIA was better than CBA because it

> is more political than scientific since there are
> likely to be various perspectives on the implications
> and desirability of a proposed development...
> Decisions regarding the use of environmental resources
> and can never be "correct", only more or less
> advantageous to the interests involved. (81)

In terms of administrative law, the most important of the provisions for EIA in the NEPA were those which gave citizens the right to prosecute proponents who had not prepared adequate impact statements. (82) According to legislators, this mechanism seemed to embody the best features of the Anglo-American legal system because it provided an accessible vehicle for review and circumvented the standing problems that had often arisen in the context of litigation.

Thus the basic philosophy was that EIA would encourage better inputs into the decision-making process and this would result in better decisions. This was a popular idea at the time. For example, as Maurer argued, it was clear that "better" information should lead to better decisions. (83) Since involving those whose lives are affected by major development projects in decisions should improve the quality of information available to decision-makers, it seemed to follow that the decisions made would also be improved.

The need for better information in decision-making had often produced diasterous results in the past. Where there are gaps in knowledge, experts and decision-makers tend to rely on past experiences, which may or may not be appropriate. (84) Environmental groups and scientists argued effectively that this is not appropriate because of synergistic interactions between forces which can produce unknown consequences. The strength of their argument was bolstered by some of the disasterous attempts to transfer first world technology to developing nations in the 1960s. (85)

Another argument for public review is that sometimes major projects may impact significantly on peoples and very little or no information is available on the nature of this impact. (86) For example, estimates for the valuation of Indian grave sites are generally unavailable and as a matter of policy most governments in Canada have not permitted development of these areas of the difficult moral problems posed by attempting to place a value on them. (87)

There were also problems with this generous philosophy. Given the danger of overloading the decision-making process with excess information, the use of general inventories and checklists as a foundation for data collection and public review proved inappropriate. (88) Thus, under American rules only relevant factors may be considered. (89) This avoids spending enormous amounts of time and money to secure opinions on different issues and hiring experts from a range of disciplines that may not have a crucial bearing on the final decision. (90)

In Canada, analogous procedures have developed. (91) For example, under the Ontario Statute, The Environmental Assessment Act (92), interest groups are confined on matters stipulated by the Minister and they will not be granted standing before either the OMB, the Environmental Assessment Board or the Joint Boards established using members of these bodies under the Consolidated Hearings Act. (93)

Not everyone in the environmental community was happy with this new attempt to "participate the public". Critics argued that EIA was merely an attempt to meet the demand for participation in decision-making and simultaneously diffuse a political time bomb. (94) In Canada, the approach taken in the United States was viewed with skepticism. As Woodrow (95) observes, Canada had never encouraged the kind of broad conservation movment that Gifford Pinchot had orchestrated in the United States. Natural resource was found on a policy of "efficient" exploitation of staples resources. Where the enviroment had arisen as an issue, the prime motivating concern was protection of human health. (95a) Moreover, the reforms eventually undertaken were not directed at these structural problems but visible irritants such as the eutrophication of lakes and air pollution in cities.

Despite this flaw in the reforms and the fact that participation clearly did not offer a solution to these structural problems, the Canadian government felt it was necesary to develop an indigenous solution to the demand for greater accountability in public decison-making on the environment. A specific federal agency, the Federal Environmental Assessment and Review Office (FEARO), would eventually be created and some of the innovations that this agency has made in the areas of public participation and intervenor funding will be considered in later sections below.

To summarize, convincing arguments were made by environmentalists and scientists that the most important way to improve decision-making on the environment was to increase public accessibility. In doing so, it was assumed that one would also facilitate public input and feedback. However, in some situations it was apparent that adjunct mechanisms such as public hearings were also required to ensure that the public had an opportunity to express their concerns about development projects. And it was on this foundation that the concept of public participation in environmental decision-making was rooted.

The Need For Intervenor Funding

If public participation is an important part of government decision-making, then a conscientious effort must be made to facilitate access to those government bodies that seek such input. Arguably one of the means to facilitate this access is intervenor funding. (96) Funding allows public interest groups that represent the public to engage experts, undertake consultations, educate their members about the project (so these members can then lobby government), make oral presentations, prepare written briefs and research complex issues. (97) In the aggregate these are important activities of any public interest group and they are usually underway in some form whether or not a group is intervening in particular projects. However, it is necessary to delineate the arguments for funding groups for participation in greater detail here.

As a preliminary point it should be noted that it is not necessarily a given that public interest groups should represent "the public" in public participation. (98) Moreover, even if they are determined to merit standing before a certain tribunal or panel, it is unclear that these groups deserve public funding to participate. At this point it is assumed that public interest interventions are a public good. Generally this assumption rests on the fact that most public interest groups usually do represent the public in an effective manner. The main argument in support of such a position is that high transaction costs prevent individual citizens from linking up and effectively representing individuals to either form a coalition or line up with an established group in order to participate in a public hearings.

The key argument in favour of intervenor funding is that it helps to overcome an enormous cost barrier to participation. This barrier has acted as a screening method in the past. The general theory behind this screening method is that only those people with serious concerns about a project or a new government policy would be willing to bear the costs of participation. (99)

The analogy that is drawn on here is litigation. Conventional wisdom holds that cost awards in Canada and other common law jurisdictions discourage litigation. (100) Similarly, forcing public interest groups to pay the costs of their participation in public hearings serves to reduce the number of parties that are willing to get involved. From the perspective of an initiating agency or a proponent, this limitation can have an important bearing on the length of the hearings and may also reduce the overall cost of the proposed project.

The screening theory does not account for the fact that Anglo-Canadian and American cost rules (100) provide a poor analog in the context of public interest hearings. In a larger percentage of public interest cases, the relief sought is not monetary; thus, neither system can provide groups with money for lawyers because the groups will not be awarded money for injunctive relief or other remedies if they are successful. (101)

In addition, the screening theory of public participation does not adequately account for numerous market failures such as the "free rider" problem. (102) According to economic theory, this occurs when individuals derive the benefit of an action without paying the cost of participating in the negotiations or efforts leading up to it. This is a frequent phenomena in the area of public interest law. While many Canadians probably endorse the actions of many public interest groups who intervene at hearings or make public displays to raise consciousness about issues, they are unwilling or unable to contribute to these groups by making donations or joining as members.

In addition to the free rider problem there are numerous structural barriers to the participation of public interest groups in hearings and other fora. These barriers will be surveyed below in order to provide support for the contention that intervenor funding is an important public good and should be supported by policy-makers.

The first structural barrier that public interest groups encounter in their effort to participate in decision-making is the preparation of professional written documents. Often these documents must be submitted before oral hearings are held. The inability of groups to assess the validity of an impact statement or policy and write an effective critique of it can act as a deterent to participation. (103)

The second structural barrier to public participation relates to oral presenations before boards and tribunals. In the past many interest groups have refused to participate in oral hearings because they lack expertise and advice on procedural matters such as cross-examination, the admissability of evidence and other aspects of legal procedure. (104) Even where lack of knowledge of procedural requirements is not technically a barrier and the board or tribunal has the power to make their own rules to suit the situation, the public interest groups may be to intimidated to participate. It must be remembered that it is usually at this stage that most media attention is focused on the evaluation of the project or policy and the stakes are very high. Some groups like Pollution Probe and Canadian Environmental Law Association (CELA) have made mistakes at these times in the past and probably would prefer not to embarass themselves any more.

Another structural barrier to public participation in Canada is the current structure of taxation. Under existing provisions, corporations can deduct almost all the costs they incur in lobbying government officials and participating at hearings for major reviews of projects. (105) This allows them to invest considerable amounts of time and energy in lobby work. In the process corporations can often stifle important reforms, as experience with tax reform in the late 1960s and early 1970s in Canada has shown so clearly. (106)

Another difficulty is that hearings often disrupt day-to-day life considerably. Where the matters involved are complex the hearings lengthy, this can prove a very significant obstactle. A good example is provided by the experience of intervenors in the EARP for the Uranium Hexafluoride plant and waste disposal facilities in Port Granby. In her book, Blind Faith, Penny Sanger vividly describes experiences of intervenors who participated in public hearings for this project. (107) She shows that intervenors lost jobs, spent considerable money on food and lodgings, irritated their families and friends and developed a pattern of psychological alienation from their communities during the hearings.(107a)

These experiences speak to the need to support individuals and groups that are willing to invest considerable energy and time in public hearings. To do otherwise is to discriminate on a class basis, in effect. The validity of this assertion is supported by the contrasting experience of different income groups in the United States with environmental litigation. In the 1950s and 1960s when this litigation became more popular as a technique for conservation and environmental protection, relatively affluent groups were often able to launch successful court challenges to decisions which might adversely impact on them. For example, in a well-known American case, wealthy land owners were able to block Consolidated Edison from constructing a large dam in upper New York State. (108)

In direct constrast, fishermen living in Newfoundland were unable to get standing in the infamous Hickey case (109) despite a demonstrable interest in the continued viability of a fishery which was wiped out by a chemical spill. One hesitates to invoke a Marxist conspiracy theory which would relate this soley to ownership of property. The relative density of population in the regions of the nation, the importance of the different economic activities involved and the attitudes of the judiciary all probably played an important role in these types of cases. However, there can be little doubt that those with money and power are able to reflect their concerns about the environment in a more effective way than their poorer counterparts.

The financial accessibility of public review hearings for major undertakings became an issue in the United States soon after the NEPA was established. (110) Since these undertaking often involve expenditures of millions of dollars and private applicants must work closely with government planners, teams of lawyers and technical experts were assembled at considerable cost for advisory purposes. It was often very clear when public hearings began how unfair and unequal this kind of scenario was.

Having outlined some of the structural barriers that face public interest groups that attempt to participate in public hearings, it is now possible to consider some of the key advantages of intervenor funding for tribunals. Half a dozen of these are identified and discussed briefly below.

Intervenor funding presents a tribunal with an opportunity to structure the submissions of the public to the extent that most of the participants in public hearings will want or need funding to make oral and written submisssions. With the flurry of public interest in participation in the late 1960s and 1970s, many tribunals attempted to open their hearing processes to the public. However, this uncontrolled public participation often complicated procedures and lengthened hearings. Moreover, some of the groups raised matters outside of the jurisdiction of the board or tribunal. As a result many administrative bodies were forced to impose time limits for presentations and limit the number of speakers. Unfortunately this has effects which deter public participation over the long-term.

Intervenor funding also affords an opportunity to encourage the formation of coalitions among interest groups. This has several advantages in terms of the overall value of public participation. Many of the presentations made to royal commissions and inquiries overlap significantly and time and money might be saved if groups were encouraged through discretionary funding to join force. For example, over 170 mining groups made submissions to the Standing Committee on Finance regarding the White paper on Tax Reform issued in 1969.(110a) Scrutiny of these submissions reveals a preponderance of similar information and analysis. It could be argued that most of these groups could have undertaken submissions jointly and, in the process, saved their corporations hundreds of thousands of dollars.

Given corporate interest in profit maximization the failure to form coalitions seems suprising and suggests that the mining industry had other intentions during the hearing process, such as making a strong and continued impact in the media. Moreover, the multitudes of mining groups who presented briefs before the Standing Committee on Finance in 1969 and 1970 were trying to make political points with both the Trudeau government and provincial governments throughout Canada. The question I would ask is this: does the acceptance of this type of pattern of participation bring into question the credibility of a panel or board which allows this kind of abuse of process? My submission is that it does and these types of abuses should be prevented whenever possible through forcing the formation of coalitions and joint submissions. However, it is noteworthy that current taxation arrangments do not encourage these kinds of coalitions and most people do not view this kind of duplication as anything more than the exercise of "speech rights."

It must be admitted that the formation of coalitions can also produce some negative consequences for public participation. When a national commission with a broad scope is undertaken, there is a need for a regional flavour in the submissions. Certainly this was evident in the submissions made to the recent Royal Commission on the Economic Union and Prospects for Canada (the Macdonald Commission). The key question is how to balance this need for a regional flavour but simultaneously not drown out other voices at public hearings by allowing the rich and powerful to maximize access to both the media and public hearings in the quise of regionalism.

Formal participation in intervenor hearings also can serve to bolster the profile of interest groups and attract new members to their cause. In fact, it could be argued that the surge of interest in environmental issues that took place in Canada during the 1970s was a reflection of the actvicism of groups such as Pollution Probe, the Canadian Nature Federation, the Canadian Arctic Resources Committee (CARC) and the National and Provicial Parks Association of Canada (NPPAC), and the Canadian Wildlife Federation (CWF). These groups all publish magazines or newsletters and they usually focus much of their analysis and discussion on recent interventions by the respective group and hearings and briefs sent to Ministers. (111)

Part of this material is intended to inform members and stir their concern about issues. However, the newsletters are also vehicles for legitimation of the interest groups and their use of donated funds. Finally, newsletters act as both an implicit or explicit mechanism to justify requests for further funding.

Intervenor funding also can act as a spur to continuous involvement in a hearing process. Lack of continuity has often posed a problem in certain jurisdictions because groups who enter the process at initial stages may drop out and others not previously involved may attempt to formally join the hearings. Either change can pose problems for proponents, especially when the latter type of group raises questions already dealt with at earlier stages, or tries to get the deficiencies already dealt with reconsidered and unecessarily delays the review hearings. (112)

Another argument for intervenor funding is that it allows groups to hire their own experts, including legal advisors. The argument for independent expertise is that professional experts often have developed their ideas in isolation from the real world. This is quite understandable; experts usually must spend a considerable amount of time and energy developing a detailed understanding of a subject (113). Having invested this much time in disciplinary training it is possible that the expert may be unable to fully communicate their views to the public or draw out the implications of a project in a frank and forthright manner. Moreover, the quest for personal legitimacy may cloud objectivity and foster an inappropriate tone in hearings. Thus, the professional expert may not have an adequate experiential basis to determine how the public will be affected by a specific project or policy. Intervenor funding allows a group to hire their own professional experts and consult with them in order to determine and evaluate social and environmental impacts. This promotes confidence in the process and allows the experts to "battle it out" without undue influence in the public hearing process and forcing the public interest groups to merely discredit government or industry scientists.

At this point it is necessary to shift gears and begin to consider some of the arguments against intervenor funding. The most frequently mentioned problem that is associated with intervenor funding is that groups often seem to have a remarkable destructive capacity. Thus, they often seem to engage in rhetorical outbursts in a staged manner to maximize media coverage and publicly embarass officials in government and industry. (114) Given the power imbalances that often exist in project planning for megaprojects, this kind of tactic seems inevitable. Moreover, it does not appear to be a convincing argument against funding because these groups perform a vital watchdog function for the Canadian public.

Another argument against intervenor funding is that it will increase competition for experts and thereby raise the overall costs of public participation. As indicated above, the present practices often necessitate considerable amount of pro bono work by lawyers and consultants. Moreover, the number of people involved in this work is not very great. In effect, the present approach tends to weed out all but those individuals who are seriously committed to social justice and environmental protection. Right now, the Canadian public is benefitting because they are "free riders" on the painstaking research and lobbying efforts of these well-intentioned lawyers and experts. (115) Therefore a significant increase in funding to more than a handful of groups might very well create an artificial market for these lawyers and experts in·the short term. (115) However, it is likely that this gap would soon be filled by other lawyers "waiting in the wings" if funding was provided on a more solid basis in the future.

A related argument that could be made is that intervenor funding will not substantially improve the content of the submissions made, even if it does help interest groups to abide by procedural requirements more stringently and make more persuasive presentations. (116) No doubt the rough-hewn perceptions of native people gave the Berger Inquiry its life and authenticity. With legal coaching the authenticity of these contributions might be undermined and the political battle for media attention lost.

Another problem one must deal with is distinguishing between legitimate public interest groups and those which are merely seeking a platform to express their views of the genral jthrust of government policies. Parallels in the legal context might well include the famous Borowski case on standing.(116a) There are numerous techniques that could be used to determine which groups is appropriate but none seem statisfactory. For example, membership numbers might give an indication of the extent of public support for the view points expressed by the group. However, if one uses membership numbers alone one might end up funding only national groups rather than local or provincial groups. This would be an unsatisfactory result in the context of a most environmental hearings. For example, hearings on the establishment of a port facility in the Northern Yukon to serve oil and gas development projects in the Beaufort Sea should involve groups representing local, regional and national interests because of the ecological significance and the economic importance of the area. (117)

Other factors that probably must be taken into account in making decisions on funding the issues that the group has expressed interest in and the historical record of the group. The importance of these matters is considered in greater detail below.

With these arguments for intervenor funding in the background, many public interest groups began to argue in a quite convincing fashion that they required intervenor funding in order to make their contribution to public policy development in Canada. These groups invaded tribunals and other pseudo-democratic arenas in the late 1960s and early 1970s in a style reminiscent of student protest activities during the period. In some cases they were taken seriously. In others, they were not.

Pollution Probe, a Toronto-based environmental group, launched the attack on the environmental front at NEB hearings on the James Bay Project in 1971. They asked embarassing questions of both the NEB and industry, arguing that it would be difficult for the NEB to judge the proposal objectively. (118) At the same time, Probe contended that interest groups should be regarded as legitimate participants in the regulatory process and that support should be provided for their work. However, the NEB ultimately rejected this argument for funding and interpreted their mandate in a limited fashion, taking advantage of technical flaws in Probe's submissions to limit the extent of participation by interest groups and the availability of cost awards. (119) In fact, it was only after the Berger Inquiry had received formal and informal presentations that the NEB agreed to accept public interest interventions as a matter of procedure on a regular basis. (120) However, the NEB has continued to refuse to make monies available to public interest groups for environmental hearings, despite convincing arguments that they have clear authority and an obligation to do so.(120a)

Since the NEB seemed unreceptive to public interest groups in this period, strategists for these groups began to employ conventional political mechanisms to have their views heard. However, Pollution Probe and other groups had set the scene. An historic breakthrough was just around the corner. All that was needed was the right forum and the right person to lead the fight for broadening support for participation and access to public hearings.

The Berger Inquiry: A Breakthrough

The initiation of planning for numerous megaprojects in both Canada and the United States in the late 1960s and the early 1970s did much to foster arguments for intervenor funding. (121) As indicated already, these projects appeared to require detailed public scrutiny and many of the structural barriers to individual and group participation described above had been encoutered. In addition, experiences with planning in Britain also suggested that serious defienciences existed in both provision of intervenor funds and opportunities to participate. (122)

Experience in the United States with public review of the Alaskan Oil Pipeline (ALESYKA) had shown the NEPA approach was not enitrely successful. In the perception of some industry and government officials, environmental groups that were opposed to the project had delayed construction of this pipeline for three years by challenging the validity and adequacy of the impact statement that had been produced for the project. (123) This proved a real windfall for American lawyers who acted on behalf of the environmental groups and would be awarded costs from the proponents. In the process a vicious cycle of dependency emerged between impact assessors and lawyers and the public interest groups. Many argued in favour of an alternative and no doubt it was this experience which eventually led a U.S. court to strike down cost awards that were being made against the proponents of large development projects. Eventually this encouraged the emergence of mediation as an alternative strategy.(123a)

In Canada the need for funding became most apparent to politicians and the academic elite during the prelude to the Mackenzie Valley Pipeline Inquiry. (124) It was apparent to these people that the process of development would be grossly unfair if funds were not provided to native groups and public interest intervenors to assess the massive proposal. Moreover, it was felt that this might pose legitimization problems. At the same time, most of these people felt that the ALEYSYKA experience should not be duplicated in the Canadian north. (125)

Berger's success in securing intervenor funding for the Inquiry was an important advance for public interest groups. Although the Terms of Reference for the Inquiry did not specifically indicate that Berger should provide intervenor funding, (127), the mandate was vague enough to allow him to interpret it creatively. In the process Berger wrote a unique chapter in Canadian history. While the importance of his efforts cannot be trivialized, it is noteworthy that his success also reflected the political climate that existed in the federal Parliament in the early 1970s, as the discussion below will show. (126)

It is important to review the background to the Berger Inquiry and the actual process in detail because it represents a turning point in Canada with respect to the value ascribed to public interest interventions. In terms of David Easton's model of decision theory (128), it could be argued that this input ultimately became the most important one in the eventual decision made by the Trudeau Liberals to reject the Mackenzie Valley Pipeline proposal. (129) It could be argued that this result defied the intent of the federal government; faced with growing energy demands and decreasing supplies of conventional reserves, the Liberals had believed it was important to plunge into frontier development.

In retrospect, the decision to fund intervenors was a minimal requirement and the intervenors probably ensured that the Trudeau Liberals did not make one of least practical development decisions in their history. Many of the aspects of the plan were unrealistic. (130) For example, both the size of the pipe and the operating pressure were greater than that of any pipeline in operation at the time (and still would be, if the pipeline had been constructed). Similarly, the total cost of the project was estimated to be over $10 billion. (131) For this reason, the Department of Finance was opposed to the project because it would have spurred inflation and drained the economy. (132)

The scale of the project was partiallly a reflection of the fact that the Mackenzie Valley pipeline proposal embodied many of the worst features of government and industrial linkage in development planning. The proposal had been spearheaded by a Task Force on Northern Oil Development that formed in 1968 after the Prudhoe Bay discovery in Alaska. (133) According to Dosman, whose book on the subject sent shock waves through federal departments in Ottawa when it was released in 1976, its "chief purpose from the first was the successful promotion of a Mackenzie pipeline corridor...." (134) Not suprisingly, the Task Force was the prime mover behind the formation of the Arctic Gas consortium. Two Crown corporations, Canada Development Corporation (CDC) and the Canadian National Railways (CNR), were involved. (135) Moreover, four of the world's largest oil companies were also members of Arctic Gas. (136) Hence, it was believed that approval of the pipeline proposed by the consortium would be a rather straight forward (and practically automatic) matter. The confidence of the consortium was evidenced by the fact that by mid 1973 Arctic Gas had spent $35 million on pipeline feasibility studies. (137) By 1977 the amount of money spent on studies had climbed to $150 million (138) despite claims that most of the information that was collected was useless in scientific terms.

With this background of government-industry linkage, it should not be surprising that public interest groups were intrigued by the plans for the Mackenzie Valley Pipeline and vocally criticized the proposal. According to many critics, the fact that the government did not approve the proposal may be primarily attributed to a curious mixture of events and the persistent criticism by these groups.

One of the most important factors in this sequence of events was the fact that the Trudeau Liberals were in a minority government at the time, relying on the support of the New Democratic Party (NDP) to continue governing. (139) The NDP had campaigned in the 1972 election on a platform that vigorously attacked perceived linkages between government and industry, specifically criticizing the Liberals for supporting "corporate welfare bums" through generous tax concessions and other grants. (140) In the process, they had elected a record number of members to the House. For this reason, the NDP believed that the Mackenzie Valley Pipeline proposal provided an excellent ground on which to criticize and potentially bring down the Liberal government.

Another factor that contibuted to this unique climate was the growth of concern about aboriginal rights. The Calder decision had been recently rendered by the Supreme Court of

Canada (141) and the James Bay Hydroelectric Project had also stimulated concern about land claims. (142) Many critics felt that it was inappropriate for the Liberals to go ahead with a large development in view of this emerging recognition for aboriginal rights and the potential environmental problems the development would cause. (143)

The federal government responded by appointing Justice Thomas Berger of the Supreme Court of British Columbia. As a lawyer and former leader of the NDP in British Columbia, Berger had demonstrated concern for both environmental and native issues. (144) Thus, his appointment was an acceptable compromise to the federal NDP caucus members who had focused so much attention on the potential impact of pipeline construction.

The intervenor funding that was provided did much to diffuse this criticism and served to give the Inquiry an aura of fairness in the eyes of the Canadian public. The public were able to follow the Inquiry because media coverage was carefully orchestrated and facilitated by Berger's staff. (145) This media coverage served to constrain the decision-making process and requir the government to account for its decision publicly. In effect, Berger ensured that the Trudeau Liberals could not get away with a whitewash. He was helped in this by the fact that the intervenor groups were articulate and made careful but critical statements to the media. For example, the speakers for the Indian and Inuit groups were often powerful and intelligent and came across well on T.V. and radio. In the print media, the Inquiry also attracted attention because the native people provided excellent human interest material. Since jounrnalists were often sympathetic to their plight, the result was that a symbiotic relationship developed between the media and the native intervenor groups. This also took place with the environmental groups, but to a lesser extent, and the experience provides strong support for the argument that public interest groups can broaden their base support through participation in public heaarings. (146)

Despite the success of the Berger Inquiry in raising consiousness about the north, intervenor funding levels were still inadequate for public interest groups. For example, Bregha (147) has observed that only one environmental group appeared before the Inquiry -- the Canadian Artic Resources Committee (CARC). While CARC made an important contribution, Bregha notes that the group "almost went bankrupt when it incurred debts of $40,000, an absurdly small sum when one considers that Foothills spent almost twice as much on NEB transcripts alone." (148) That CARC did not go bankrupt may be attributed to the fact that it gained a solid reputation during the Berger Inquiry and has maintained its prominence through continued participation in many heaings in and on the north since then.

In the end the predictions of public interest intervenors that the match would prove to be a "David and Goliath" contest were borne out by the actual experience of the Inquiry itself. As Bregha has observed, "the combined resources of the public interest groups amounted to roughly one-tenth of one percent of Canadian Artic Gas's expenditures during its five year existence." (159) Bregha's figures are somewhat misleading because the intervenors were often able to work together (e.g. sharing transcripts) and the Canadian university community funded an enormous amount of the research that was presented at the Berger hearings. However, the experience of CARC and other groups during the Berger Inquiry showed that groups which could not draw on the resources and DIAND and other federal programs for technical and financial support could probably not afford to effectively participate in northern hearings.

It could be argued that one of the negative results of intervenor funding for Berger is that it merely shifted the forum of debate about many public policy issues northward. Social and nationalist groups that had been outwitted by the quick-footed and shifty Trudeau Liberals found a new audience in the north and another way to access the national media in Canada and express their concerns. As Professor Robert Page, spokesperson for one of these groups, admitted in his retrospective book on the Inquiry (149), many of the claims made were inflated and somewhat misleading. This probably reflects frustration with the lack of participation in numerous policy and regulatory decisions over the preceding decade. However, with the benefit of hindsight it is possible to see this controversy as a transplanted battle between industrial forces and counter-culture groups that were advocating alternatives to the staples model of development that had prevailed since the fur trade. (150) Whether such a battle could have been avoided entirely is doubtful. (151) Nevertheless, it is questionable whether funding such a transplanted debate is an effective use of scarce government resources.

Undoubtedly, the decision made at the beginning of the Berger Inquiry to involve the public as fully as possible influenced the outcome of the process significantly. The participation strategies and the programmes of public education associated with the Inquiry generated considerable support for the "no-development" option that Berger recommended. (152)

Intervenor funding also shaped the outcome of the NEB hearings because the success of groups with the Berger Inquiry motivated many groups to continue their interventions. (153) The results of their work also appear to have paid off. Due to the strenous work of intervenor groups working on small budgets and deep commitment, the NEB was forced to acknowledge tht serious environmental and socio-economic problems would be created by construction of the Mackenzie Valley Pipeline. (154) As a result of the evidence these groups presented (155) the NEB concluded "that the [Canadian Arctic Gas Pipeline] prime route...would be environmentally unacceptable..." (156) Although the NEB decision did not rule out construction of alternative routes, sections of the pipeline that could have damaged sensitive parts of the Northern Yukon coast and Mackenzie Delta were judged technically difficult. (157) This was a small victory for the public interest intervenors but it should not be simplistically dismissed.

As Dosman has argued this unique type of public review could very well have proven to be a proverbial "flash in the pan." He argued in 1976 that the Berger Inquiry was an anomaly and that it would never be repeated again.(157a) However, on this point he was clearly wrong. The measure of social justice that intervenor funding and wide public participation had provided to the Berger Inquiry would inspire many other similar commissions, inquiries and debates over the next decade as we will see below.

The impact of the Berger Inquiry on public policy is difficult to guage. In 1974 the Trudeau government had permitted drilling in the Beaufort Sea with no public review in anticipation of pipeline construction and a major energy crisis. By 1977 the energy crisis had dissolved and the need for costly energy from the Arctic had declined. Consequently some have argued that Berger had no effect whatsoever on the decision that was taken.

However, this argument is not entirely persuasive. It is clear that Trudeau was committed to Diefenbaker's "northern vision" of Canada. Within three years of the Berger Report's release, the Liberal Cabinet in Ottawa had approved a pre-build of the Mackenzie Valley pipeline to Norman Wells (158) as a harbinger to their ill-fated National Energy Program. In the process, it is clear that the federal government violated the spirit of their promise to abide by the recommendations in the Berger Inquiry made after the Inquiry report was released in 1977. Thus, it could be argued that the key results of the Inquiry was that public attitudes as to what constituted a fair process for assessing a major public project had been altered by the Inquiry.

Not everyone was happy with the increased access to public policy-making that Berger had facilitated. Critics of the intervenor funding program argued that it had not significantly improved the effectiveness of the interventions that were made. (160) Moreover, they contended that most of the important points that were made about environmental problems relied on reports prepared by technical experts in government departments. Finally, it was contended that in an era of fiscal restraint the country could not afford such an innovation in social policy. (161)

The validity of these arguments seems questionable. the first argument that the fundind did not imporve the quality of interventions is difficult to evaluate, primarily because effectiveness of the interventions can only be assessed in terms of a particular ideological framework. While the second point is indsputable, the argument offered is not convincing. The importance of public interest interventions is not merely that they offer information. Irtervenors ascribe values to the information already available to the public and make it relevant to policy-makers in the process. The last point was refuted by the very fact that governments all over the world felt that this innovation in social policy was essential, even in an era of fiscal restraint, and would attempt to emulate the Berger Inquiry over the next decade, as we will see below.

Berger's influence on perceptions of the need for greater public participation in environmetal and social decision-making was much broader than he might have predicted at the outset. (162) The model he and his staff had developed was studied with enthusiasm at Canadian universities and abroad and the results of his work became widely known to the international community of impact assessors. (163) For this reason perhaps it is not suprising that the model for public participation adopted in the World Conservation Strategy (164) reflected Berger's approach.

The first provincial government prompted to respond to these increased demands for participation was Progressive Conservative Minority in Ontario. (165) The parallels to the events that led up to the establishement of the Berger Inquiry are remarkable. a major disposition of northern lands for logging had been proposed and the benefactor as the English multinational, the Reed Paper company. Native groups raised environmental and social concerns and threatened violence if these problems were not addressed. In response the Ontario government established a Royal commission on the Northern Environment headed by Justice Patrick Hartt. Like Berger, Hartt interpreted his mandate broadly and provided intervenors with funding. The basic objective of the public participation was to ensure that the final report and recommendations of the commission reflect the opinions of the people living int eh North. The Commission considered the objective was attainable if financial assistance was available to help groups and individuals participate in the work of the Commission. (166)

As noted aleready, the controversy that the Berger Inquiry had generated in Canada required the NEB to take a new approach to intervenor participation. Historically, the NEB regarded "real intervenors" as the major players in the oil and gas or electricity industry. (167) After Berger, this body made a significant policy shift and began to give groups standing on a regular basis.(168) While the comparitive receptivity of the NEB has been welcomed, the reluctance of this tribunal to financially support groups by awarding costs is lamented by Ian Blue in his review of the Inuit intervention in hearings for the Arctic Pilot Project. (169)

In the result it is clear that Berger had a tremendous impact on the future of intervenor funding for public participation in Canada. Arguably this impact has been felt mostly in the area of environmental decision-making. In the next section of the legacy of Berger will be considered in terms of a specific federal policy in this area, the Environmental Assessment and Review Process (EARP).

The Federal Response in Canada

The federal government in Canada responded in diverse ways to the increased demands for public participation.

The first response of the federal government in Canada was the creation of the Environment in 1971. In addition, certain researchers and policy-makers were mandated tio begin exploring the idea of a Canadian model for EIA in 1972. This investigation culminated in the establishment of the Environmental Assessment

and Review Process in December 1973. (170) EARP was inteded to
deal with federal projects (171) but was not provided with a
statutory basis. (172)

The emerging Canadian philosophy on EIA was that the
American experience should be avoided. The Hon. Jack Davis, in
announcing the establishment of the EARP on March 14, 1974,
alluded to the tangled legal battles that had occured in Alaska
in a speech to the House:

> I hope...that we can avoid delays and other
> pitfalls which a strictly legalistic approach would
> causse in this country...We will not hold up
> developments which are clean from an environmental
> point of view and, ..., we will not jbring the
> environmental assessment into disrepute. (173)

Admionistrators in FEARO interpretated this as a mandate to
develop the environmental assessment process in a unique and
creative way and this development continues even today. (174) In
essence, EARP requires the sponsors of major projects -- called
. proponents or initiating department -- to ensure that
enfironmental and social impacts aare taken into account in the
planning process. (175) Accordingly, proponents are required to
screen their projects and determine whether they will have
impacts; if they do, it is expected that the proponent will
prepare an EIS for public review. (176)

If public review is deemed necessary, then the Minister of
Environment, after consultatiion with the Minister responsible
for the initiating department, appoints the members of the panel
and issues terms of reference outlining the scope of the public
review. (177) The EIS provides the basis for the public recview,

and all panel hearings are conducted in non-judicial manner.

The fact that the EARP does not have a legislative basis has bveen questioned by Lucas, Maclead and Miller in a review of procedures and policies relaated to regulation of High Arctic Development. (178)

Similarly, various federal ministers os the environment have decried the lack of procedures. In 1980, John Fraser, then the Minister of the Environment under the short-lived Conservative government said; in reflecting on a proposal to drill in Lancaster Sound, the following:

> I think that the Environmental Process should be mandatory. The present Minister [of DIAND] may have a lot of good will, but I don't know about the next Minister ... I'm anxious to establish a regime backed by the law that will last for decades and not just through the good will of one Minister or another. (179)

Fraser was unable to make good on his promise to provide a legal basis for the EARP. Morover, a series of Liberal Ministers of the environment were unable to garner the necessary attention and funding to make the matter or priority. thuys, it was not until recently that revamping in EARP became a major issue once again. (180)

The argument for entrenching EARPas a legislated process is not entirely convincing however. (181) As Emond observer, "[w]hatever one may say about EIA, its success is more related to the people who adminster the process and the politician, and has little to do with the existence of legislation." (182) In retrospect, Emond'd observation has been borne out by experiences in Canada and the United States over the past decade. In the analysis below it will become apparent that the flexibility permitted to FEARO administrators has allowed them to encourage high levels of public participation over the past decade.

One of the strongest arguments for intervenor funding for the EARP is the lax standard of proof that the proponent must meet. Generally it has been shown that most EIAs presented to panels have failed to even meet marginal criteria in terms of conventional methods of risk analysis and scientific evaluation of ecological impacts. (183) Public participation in the evaluation of the EIAs has served to keep both the proponenets and the sponsoring agencies honest about the quality of the research upon which predictions are based and the need for further work.

The Berger Inquiry set an important precedent for northern pipeline hearings. As a result, the Alaska Highway Pipeline Inquiry headed by K. Lysyk (184) also made intervenor funding availabe. The report that was eventually produced by the Inquiry recommended the establishement of a Northern Pipeline Agency to regulate the construction of the pipeline that the Trudeau Liberals had endorsed in principle.

The extent to which this difference form influenced the outcome of the Lysyk inquiry is unclear. (185) Like the Berger inquiry, the Alask Highway pipeline project review recommendced construction prior to settlement of land claims. Moreover, the report also outlined in considerable detail the necessary steps that shouls be taken to minimize impacts of development on Yukon communities. (186) However, the tone of the rports was much more conservative and irs focus on the need to establish an agency to regulate construction of the eventual pipeline represented a departure from the anti-development thrust of the Berger report.

The structure and process of the proposed Agency was intervenor funding for participants. Moreover, the Minister responsible for DIAND at the time, Hugh Faulkner, acknowlededtged in reflections on his experiences that native groups and public interest intervenors had contributed significantly to Cabinet's decision to approve the concept. (187) However, the general thrust of the northern inquiries that followed Berger

One fundamental difference bvetween the Berger and Lysyk inqurries noted already was the abgreviated length of the latter. (188) As a result the amount of research available at the time of the Lysyk inquiry was comparatively sparse. Moreover, it was not possible to coordinate political education activities and local community interventions to the same degree in the Yukon or garner wide media attention. The Canadian public had already consumed its fill of northern inquaries in the preceeding three years.

This experience provides an interesting contrast to the Berger process because it was reactive -- both to Berger's work and the proponent's application. In view of some people, experience argues against this reactive model of public participation. At the same time there are others who felt this EARP had many positive features, including the relatively shortened review period and the more "objective" assessment of potential environmental problems. (189)

Following the Lysyk Inquiry, few northern environmental assessment processes were funded to the same degree. In general it appeared that Dodman's prohecies regarding the likelihood of repetition of another Berger Inquiry were accurate. (190) Moreover, interest in northern development waned and the media began to focus on other importan public policy issues.

Inquiries related to development in Lancaster Sound served to once again bring these descrepancies to light (191) A series of CBC New Items on the planning process, a "Nature of Things" television show and other visibvle media focussed on the inequities of the planning process and the need for support of native groups and public interest groups.

The recommendation of the Lancaster Sound Panel brought out the potential difficulties inherent in a complex review of environmental impacts in its Supplementary Recommendations. (5.6)

> (i) The Proponent showed little effectiveness in public communications. Initiating departments should provide assistance and a clear direction to proponents during all phases of the public information program.

> (ii) throughout the hearings, requests were made for jpublic funding by various intervenors attending the hearings. the Panel recommends that [FEARO] should develop a mechanism for the provision of public funds to enable intervenors to adequately prepare for public hearings. (192)

The Lancaster Sound Panel also made the following assertion with respect to the need for regional planning:

> .. the Panel concludes that a much broader review is required of the present and future uses of Lancaster sound, in order to avoid committing Canada to a course of action prejudicial to the optimum conservation and utilization of all resources in the area. the questiions potentially conflicting resource uses must be identified, and thus the desire of the local residents to participate in the development of resource use strategies. The Panel supports their participation and recommends that a comprehensive review be carried out as soon as possible of potential resosurce uses of the Lancaster Sound area. (193)

Fortunately the Panel's recommendation did not fall on deaf ears and over the next four years a detailed public planning exercize was undertaken in the Sound region. (194) This model has served to illustrate th need for a comprehensive land use planning process in both the northern territories (195). In this process, public participation is formalized through representation of the different interest groups on the planning panels in a manner which emulates models employed in other areas. (196)

In its juxtaposition of these two aspects of the Lancaster Sound review, the panel presented FEARO with support it required DINA for greater funding of public intervenor groups. If the requiste informatiion requirements had been fulfilled, it is possible that the argument for intervenor funding would have been less persuasive. In the circumstances it is apparent that DINA was left with little choice. Funding the Beaufort intervenors beame a necessary legitmization for a process that was far beyond the scope of a normal EARP.

Bureaucrats in FEARO responded accordingly. Compared with earlier EARPS, the Beaufort process represented an impressive attempt to involve the public in a major development proposal. The changes made in the process could be viewed as approaching the partnership model of decisiion-making advocated by Arnstein. However, the most progressive feature of the Beaufort EARP was provision of intervenor funding. In this sennse, it was reminiscent of the Berger Inquiry, and indeed, reflected many of the tensions apparent in previous northern development proposal debates.

There was a clear tension in the initial planning for the Beaufort Inquiry, as statements made by FEARO officials prior to the hearings suggest. For example, Ewan Cotterill, Executive Chairman of FEARO in 1981 and an employee of Dome Petroleum during the hearings, told an Arctic Petroleum Operator's Association Conference in 1981 that the government had to simultaneously accomodate demands for participation from public interest groups and somehow streamline the planning process for industry. (197)

As with the Berger Inquiry, reconciling these two disparate goals was necessary for legitimation reasons. (198) The reconciliation offered by the federal Liberal government was to fund intense public participation for input into the decision that would eventually have to be taken to develop Beaufort oil and gas at an accelerated rate.

In order to avoid the confrontations that emerged in the course of the Berger Inquiry, a pro-active approach to planning was taken. (199) Accordingly, an issues seminar was held in Calgary on September 30, 1980. This location was chosen because early consulltation (200) had revealed this was the central location for most groups. At the issues seminar, presentations were made and a discussion was held on the plans outlined by the proponent. Transcripts of this discussion were eventually distrbuted to all registerd participants.

The next stage in the Beaufort EARP involved a series of visit to 26 northern communities to tell representatives about upcoming activities and distribute more information. (201) Interpreters were used to ensure that Inuit and Dene peoples could get the information and provide feedback. Moreover, panel publications and bulletins were issued in Inuit dialects.

Over the course of the next year other changes were made to the EARP in response to requests from the groups. A local office was opened in Inuvik, staffed by a native northerner. In addition, the Panel secretariat made a concerted effort to maintain contact with all participating and affected groups, as well as government agencies.

Draft guidelines for the EIS were ultimately issued and widely distributed in the Fall of 1981. Public meetings were held to review the draft guidelines in eight northern communities in November and December, 1981. Final guidelines were issued soon after these meetings and sent to all participants. (202)

Using these guidelnes, the proponents produced a seven volume EIS which was more than 2000 pages in length.

Public interest groups were provided with ample opportunities to comment on the EIS and in view of the compendia of submissions to the Panel, obviously took advantage of them. (203) In response to deficiencies identified in the written submissions, the Panel issued an interim report which directed the proponents to produce additional documentation. The final documents were provided in August 1983 and the hearings were held in the Fall of 1983.

The Panel issued its final report in July of 1984, recommending that development could proceed if certain guidelines were followed and federal agencies worked closely with both the oil companies and native groups to minimize environmental and social impacts. (204) However, many groups were not happy with the overall outcome of the EARP because they felt that the public participation amounted to a legitimation of federal policies in the north, rather than a challenge to them. (205)

The most important innovatiion of the Beaufort EARP was that it was the first federal environmental decision-making process which made significant amounts of funding avalable for public review. (207) FEARO was unable to obtain the money required for its own intervenor funding program in this case but DIAND made funds available to the agency on an experimental basis. (207)

To ensure a degree of fairness in the allocation process, the decisions were made by a committee of four people set up independently of the Panel. Research conducted for DIAND evaluating the program suggests that most people associated with the Beaufort EARP felt the funding committee was independent and allocated the monely in a fair way. (208)

The total expenditures for the Beaufort EARP were $3.8 million. (209) Of this amount, approximately $1 million was spent on intervenor funding. The money was divided among 32 recipient groups as shown in Table 1. As the Table shows, the leading six groups received 72% of the funds distributed. The other contributions were smaller, most in the range of ten thousand dollars or less with an average of $950. The money was used by the large groups to pay for detailed research and consulted work on many aspects of the Beaufort EIS and alternative development strategies.

The smaller contributions were used primarily to fund local research projects in communities, travel to hearings, and other consultation expenses. It is interesting to note that during the course of the Inquiry a peerception arose among many people in FEARO and on the Panel that much better value was obtained by funding the latter groups rather than the former. (210) This may related in part to the ideological biases of individuals working with the large native organizations and public interest groups. (211)

In the eyes of most people who knew about the programme, the intervenor funding provided for the Beaufort EARP was a success. The effect of the funding was to bolster to participation in the decision and educate northerners about the decvelopment plans. Arguably many of the goals outlined in the Logic Chart for public participation and intervenor funding were achieved in the Beaufort Inquiry. (see Figure 6). However, it should be noted that the key public interest group working on the Canadian North was forced to drop out of the public interest coalition effort because they perceived the money made available was inadequate. (212)

According to an evaluation of the intervenor funding program prepared by Boreal Engineering, several unintended consequences also arose. The following unintended effects were identified:

1. Greater public awareness of government and their intentions.

2. Raised expectations. Funding intervenor raised their expectations about the role of public participation in the decision-making. (EARP is strictly advisory).

3. Repetitious interventions were made.

4. Money was spent on interventions outside the well outside of scope of the panel.

5. Increased delays and high regulatory costs for the proponents were apparent.

6. A greater degree of social consensus was achieved on the need for a smaller scale development project.

7. Related to (6) is the perception that future litigation would be prevented because a social consensus emerged on the need for development. (213)

Whether these unintended consequences hould be viewed in a negative way is unclear. Many would argue that these kinds of gaps and overlaps in the planning process will appear whether or not bureaucrats admit it. As with the Berger Inquiry, public participation in this case served to ensure that potential problems that might have arisen and could be anticipated to arise if the project had gone ahead were dealt with and monitored if they could not be fully mitigated.

Summary

In reflection on public participation in environmental assessment in Canada over the past decade, it is apparent that the legitimacy of the process has been determined in part by the amounts of intervenor funding that has been provided. The EARP administrators have recognized this and accordingly embarked on an innovative program of funding intervenor groups. This pattern continues in the recent program for funding intervenors to the Labrador hearings.

Reaction, Retrenchment and NIMBY

As the discussion above has already suggested, increased public participation has not been well received by some administrators. (215) In fact, it could be argued that while the state has provided funding to intervenor groups it has done so reluctantly and often without the support of planners. (216) These planners have often argued that complex methodological problems would arise if public participation were encouraged. (217) To a certain degree, they have been vindicated by the emergence of wide-spread phenomena such as the Not-in-My-Backyard (NIMBY) syndrome. In this section, the response of the bureaucracy to problems such as NIMBY is explored.

As a point of departure it is important to recognize that awareness of the need for participation and attitudes of the public towards politics usually narrow the potential range of participants in decision-making considerably. Kasperson (218) contends that most often the public has little knowledge of resource development conflicts and consequently have little impact on decision-making. Even if the public is aware of the issues, sometimes the problem can appear excessively complex and bureaucrats may find it difficult to make public hearings accessible. The Tax Reform debate in Canada in the late 1960s provides an excellent example. Tax policy seemed excessively complex at the time and despite arguments made that tax policy was too important to be left to politicians and bureaucrats, the Canadian political system refused to respond and provide a broad

The reasons for this refusal are unclear. However, it could be argued that bureaucratic resistance played an essential role. Expanded public participation has not thrilled certain administrators and environmental managers. Invariably they tend to invoke arguments similar to those surveyed in our discussion of the genesis of the modern industrial state. (219) Some academic commentators have claimed that when the conflict is structural in nature, participation may only delay an important decision as politicians attempt to promote public support or avoid an unpopular decision before an election. (220)

An example of this would be the controversy over siting of industrial waste facilities in southern Ontario by the Ontario Waste Management Corporation (OWMC). The need for this facility has been apparent for more than a decade. However, it was not until the early 1980s that the Ontario government began to explore different options and sites for construction of a disposal plant. At that time, a site was selected in South Cayuga. After strong public outcry, sparked in part by poor planning for the facility, the government decided to take a different approach and established the OWMC in 1983. Its mandate is to find a suitable site as soon as possible. One of the concessions made to public interest groups like CELA in order to speed up the process was that intervenor funding would be provided to ensure the site eventually proposed was realistic and sensible.

To date, one wonders whether the Liberal government at Queen's Park regrets the generosity of their predecessors in providing this money. Public participation has mainly served to block the plans of the OWMC to build at a site in West Lincoln and raise options and alternatives which presently can not be implemented now (e.g. reduced waste production, recycling) because they require long-term shifts in attitudes towards consumption and lifestyles. Thus, intervenor funding in this case has served to delay construction of *a government-supported* waste facility and fueled an active NIMBY group. (221)

Similar problems have been encountered in the attempt to site transmission lines in southern Ontario. (222) Opponents tend to take the position that their personal interests to an aesthetic environment should take precedence over consumer needs for electricity and exporting electricity to the Northern United States.

These NIMBY phenomena have caused growing retrenchment in the area of enviromental planning. According to some environmental planners, these patterns of citizen activism speak to the need for more sophisticated techniques for managing the issues that arise from development projects. (223) Moreover, many argue in favour of limiting participation and steamlining proposals. This argument appears to have influenced many governments in Canada and other industrial nations in the late 1970s. (224) For example, the Conservative government in Ontario felt it was necessary to enact "fast-track" legislation because of the possibility of overlap between the EAA and the Planning

Act and the fact that public review of certain projects might delay projects. This response seems remarkable in view of the actual structure of Ontario's EAA. Under section 7 of that statute, requests for public involvement are carefully screened by advisers to the Minister of the Environment and only rarely are inquiries held, leading some commentators to claim recently that the EAA is getting rusty form its lack of use. (225) Accordingly, it could be argued that Ontario's fast-track legislation was primarily symbolic and intended to appease potential investors scared off by the rhetoric of the ORCNE and other environmental inquiries in Canada.

Uncertainty is an inherent aspect of EIA (227) and this has also been invoked by planners and administrators to argue in favour of limiting public participation in certain cases. Where gaps in information are large and attempting impact prediction is difficult, public participation may make the decision-making process more complicated. (228) In these cases environmental groups may couch their opinions in terms of "maybes" rather than clear options. For example, they might endorse a northern pipeline project if evidence supported a certain level of impact on wolves but advocate an alternative if the level of impact exceeded a threshold which would lead to a decline of the wolf population over a long period. However, this type of contribution to the public hearing process may be difficult to integrate into a decision-making process because of uncertainties about the potential for mitigation or synergistic effects of the proposal. Where many groups make similar interventions and propose numerous alternatives on many different social and environmental matters, the potential for confusion seems enormous. (229) Moreover, aggregation of the encyclopaedic information that this approach generates is wasteful and inappropriate, as the Berger Inquiry showed so clearly.(229a)

Other arguments have also been offered against public participation in reaction to the NIMBY syndrome. Some planners doubt the value and necessity of local interpretations of government initiatives. While it is true that environmental decisions usually hinge on local considerations, they argue that many of the opinions offered by public interest groups are predictable and often boil down to opposition based on personal economic interests.(230) For example, a widespread phenomena in North America has been opposition to locating group homes for mentally-retarded children and ex-convicts in certain middle class neighborhoods on the grounds that these homes lower property values and alter the character of the area. Recently, it has been shown that these arguments are largely unfounded.(230a) Thus, to allow groups of citizens to oppose the public agencies that wish to cite these facilities in these neighbourhoods seems unrealistic.

This discussion shows that public participation is not a panacea for decision-makers. Ultimately someone must determine what weight to give to the views of the public and how to use the information contributed in a creative and meaningful way. (231) Thus, an adjunct argument is sometimes made in favour of investing money in educating and sensitizing bureaucrats and politicians as an alternative to funding public participation. This is a view espoused by the authors of the World Conservation Strategy, a United Nations Project undertaken in 1980 which was influenced by the Berger Inquiry. According to the WCS authors, Third World nations can begin to implement more sensitive policies on the environment when bureaucrats in government agencies become familiar with the need for integrating conservation and development. (232)

Of course, employing this approach might merely increase the power of bureaucrats and create an environmental technocracy in the Third World. Ideally it would be best to implement both increased funding for intervenor groups and improve education programs for bureaucrats so they can learn to use the information generated by the public in a more effective way. It is clear that many bureaucrats get a real education in accountability and responsibility when they are forced to answer to the concerns of intervenor groups in public hearings. (233) On the balance these arguments for simplified decision-making do not seem to effectively counter the case that has been made for public participation.

Another argument that is sometimes made against public participation is that environmentalists are merely ideologues. This argument has been made in convincing terms by Wengert, in reviewing his experience with water projects in the United States. (234) Wengert argues that some environmentalists are "squawkers" and they adhere to "dogmatism with which hostile points of view are asserted, often in the face of weak data."

(235) He goes on to state

> I have been amazed at the failure of many places
> to recognize the destructive potential of the rhetoric
> and polemic of citizen participation when it is not
> dealt with in operational terms but used simply to
> discredit the existing system and to highlight its
> deficiencies without suggesting constrtuctive changes
> or comparing the situation with realizable
> alternatives. (236)

Arguably Wengert's points support the proposition that groups should be funded so that their work can be more systematic rather than polemical. If the predictions and worst case scenarios outlined by environmental groups often seem outrageous, usually they reflect intuitions and experiences rather than research. In fact, one could argue that it is remarkable that these intervenors have been right about their intuitions so often. Clearly if public interest groups received more support this problem would be partially alleviated. As the discussion of the Berger Inquiry has already indicated, when money has been made available, the contributions of public interest groups, native organizations and NGOs have been truly remarkable.

According to Wengert, there are also serious problems with determining who should participate. He challenges the doctrine applied in water resources management, based on "significantly affected" test. (237) Implicit in his critique is an argument that only those people with a clear financial interest or representing a groups of people with such an interest should be involved formally in public hearings. In terms of equity and most public policy issues in Canada, this clearly is a simplistic argument. It has been shown repeatedly over the past decade that public decisions must be viewed in a holistic light. To do otherwise is to reduce them to compartmentalized and isolated matters and return to a pre-1960s mentality. Thus, it seems inevitable that one must reject Wengert argument for applying this type of test out of hand.

Whether Wengert's other arguments should be granted credence is unclear. In some respects, he and other critics of public involvement have taken up the mantle of Schumpeter and other political theorists who were skeptical about the value and need for public participation. It does not seem desirable to return to the "realism" they advocated then as a solution to the modern problems faced by decision-makers.

In addition to the critique offered by planners, Marxists and critical theorists have also lambasted public participation as a legitimation response. (238) Best know is the critical theorist, Jurgen Habermas, author of the well-known tract, Legitimation Crisis. (239) His work suggests that participation is an attempt to diffuse contraditions in modern capitalist society and give the illusion of power to people. He does not hold much optimism about the potential of this participation to transform the structural problems that are evidenced in these debates over public policy. Moreover, Habermas contends that this participation has been undertaken to legitimate capitalist relations of production and he doubts the value of this approach over the long-term.

Another critic of public participation in governmental decison-making is George Swazblowski. (230) He argues that it is difficult to achieve an optimal level of public participation in the modern state because technological rationiality poses a fundamental contradiction:

> ..governments face an insurmountable dilemma, a fundamental contradiction between imperatives of technological rationality and such values as increased openess and wider access to the policy-making units...I submit that this contradiction cannot be resolved. Technological rationality demands the eventual creation of a totally integrated decisional system.... In such a system, the goals of efficiency, effectiveness and productivity would dominate over all other values, including those of participation, openess and wide access to public decison-making. (241)

Following this argument, we must conclude that intervenor funding alone is only a small step in improving the decision-making process. The paradigm of instrumental rationality that underlies industral culture must also be challenged. Moreover, the public must be educated for participation and advocacy if they are to do this effectively.

Despite the areguments of Habermas and Swazblowski, it is not clear that public participation has not positively influenced decision-making in Canada. Indeed, public interest groups can claim that the results of the Berger Inquiry and other environmental hearings have demonstrated the importance of both public participation andd intervenor funding. In most cases the increased awareness that the hearings have generated has ensured that unrealistic development proposals have not gone ahead. Moreover, if the projects have been approved, often the contributions of public interest groups have ensured that proper mitigation measures were implemented for both environmental and social impacts flowing from the project.

In terms of native participation, this argument is less persuasive. In the early 1970s native groups in Canada often argued that their constituencies would be maginalized by large development projects in the same way that the CPR had wrought destruction of the lifeway of Prairie Indians. (242) On this ground they sought intervenor funding to prevent this trend of marginalization and were largely successful in making their case at many hearings, usually with the help of sympathetic southern public interest intervenors and academics. The match was invariably portrayed as the bad white men wronging noble savages and it was difficult for politicians to argue otherwise in view of the socio-economic circumstances facing most native people in Canada.

While this kind of portrayal worked well throughout the 1970s, it is unclear whether it will continue to succeed in the future. Over the past decade, native people have begun to undertake their own development projects. Already serious divisions have appeared in the relationships between environmental NGOs and native organizations over the fur trapping issue. It seems likely that these kinds of divisions will continue to grow in the future. Moreover, as the discussion in the introduction of this paper suggested, there is discontent among certain bureaucrats about how money which is being given to native groups is actually spent. The big question seems to be this: can native groups use the money to challenge the ideological framework of modern industrialism capitalism in arguing for the reforms they seek? The answer emanating from Ottawa at present would appear to be no.

Part of the problem with intervenor funding for native groups stems from the fact that the money has been provided to allow native groups to <u>perceive</u> that they have a degree of control over development. The reality, of course, is that intervenor funding can do no more than this. Without internal sources of expertise, native groups have been forced to rely on the research of other agencies and individuals.

In the long run native groups must counter this by developing their own projects and beginning to dictate the agenda of development in the Canadian hinterland. The Berger Inquiry and other subsequent inquiries has shown this to be the case. In addition they must become partners in development decisions through joint ventures with government and the private sector. To this end, it is apparent that most corporations did not seriously consider native groups as potential partners in development proposal until very recently.

To summarize the analysis above, it is apparent that public participation in environmental decison-making does not mean much without funding. In fact, it could be argued that such participation is a symbolic use of politics. (243) According to Murray Edelman, this is a process which meshes deep-seated popular attachment sot authority and protectiveness together with symbols of government action. Public hearings and government presentations successfully deflect demands for structural change in our socio-economic fabric. Equivalences with the pollution of aboriginal lands, mass unemployment, racism, sexual inequality and a host of other issues are obscured. (244) Intervenors can rarely make connections between these issues effectively and persuasively without public funding. In contrast, the Berger Inquiry served to show that the convergences between these issues can be drawn out more effectively with government support. The difficulty is that this kind of participation tends to frighten most administrators and politicians because it is difficult to "manage."

There are other reasons to support intervenor funding however. Increasing federal support for public interest interventions will probably improve decision-making over the long-term. Thus, federal agencies should react to the demand for greater accountability in their regulatory practices by establishing a new legislative basis for funding public interest groups and responding to the recent decisions of the Canadian courts against awarding costs to certain groups. (245)

The exact impact that such a strengthened legislative base could have on policies and practices related to environmental protection in Canada is unclear, however. Reforms to process are important. The problem is that most of the key project and policy decisions which affect the environment are made at the regional and provincial levels and involve decisions on land use, recycling and other local issues. Unfortunately, most provincial governments have not demonstrated much enthusiasm for funding intervenor groups to participate in the reform of policies in these areas, despite Ontario's recent innovations. (246) This raises the question as to whether federal money should be used to support public interest groups in local and regional decisions, especially when they are of a scope analogous to the Beaufort EARP. Unfortunately, the constitutional issues that this type of funding would raise might scuttle such an effort and it is doubtful such an approach would find favour in the courts today.(246a)

The alternative option is to strengthen the federal role in environmental decision-making through improving existing legislation. With the recently announced Environmental Protection Act (247) it is clear the federal government is moving in this direction. However, the proposed statue has been widely criticized by environmental groups and CELA as primarily symbolic, with little actual provision for increased public participation in regulatory decision-making.

Another factor that may influence the future of intervenor funding in Canada is the current movement in the industrialized West towards deregulation. According to those who support this movement to dismantle many government agencies, deregulation would save taxpayers and industry billions of dollars every year by reducing the amount of paper work that these agencies generate. (248)

While the mania for deregulation also spilled over into other areas in the early 1980s due to the election of conservative regimes in the United States and Britain, it is unclear whether it should be applied in them. (249) In the area of social policy, deregulation has implied movement away from interventionist government policies and programmes in employment, health and housing. According to some crttics this has produced a surge of homeless, poor and sick people in the United States. Moreover, this type of approach to social policy would violate the spirit of Canada's historical commitment to redistribution and regional equity.

In the environmental area, deregulation (and weak historical patterns of regulation of pollution) has also produced negative effects in the United States and some of these continue to spill over into Ontario (via Niagara Falls) and drift into Eastern Canada in the form of Acid Rain. For this reason perhaps it should not be surprising that the recent Macdonald Commission called for increased regulation of industry to protect the Canadian environment. (250)

These patterns of public concern suggest that there will be a need to increase rather than decrease the amount of funding available to public interest groups in the next decade. These groups must act as a watchdog for governments throughout Canada in this era of fiscal restraint. Since it is likely that restraint will be institutionalized in the new equalization arrangements negotiated between the federal government and the provinces, the need to support these groups will continue to grow rather than decline over the next decade.

An Overview of Different Approaches to Intevenor Funding

In view of the various models of public participation outlined by Arnstein (251) and discussed above, it is possible to envision a number of methods to support intervenor groups. This section will survey some of the mehtods that can be employed and outline a proposed set of criteria for determining which groups should be funded.

As a preliminary matter it is first necessary to consider what the role of lawyers should be in the inquiry process and the relationship between tribunals, public interest groups and lawyers. This issue has already been touched upon in relation to the development of the EARP in Canada. As was noted in the previous section, an attempt was made to minimize the role of lawyers in this process and this pattern continues today.

The reasons for this are really quite simple. One of the almost popular arguements against intervenor funding is that most of the money ends up in the hands of lawyers. Certainly this has been the case with respect to numerous regulatory proceedings on environmental matters over the past two decades and also applies to the experience of the federal and provincial bodies in Canada. The result is that lawyers are often perceived as the high priests of regulation. (252) While efforts have been made in many public inquiries in Canada to downplay the role of lawyers (253), it is clear that they still tend to dominate many public proceedings.

If lawyers seem unpopular and unfairly criticised by public interest groups, they only have themselves to blame. Lawyers did not develop a good reputation in the early days of environmental assessment, primarily because they seemed preoccupied with doing three things:

1. establishing the credibility of witnesses. Many scientists and citizen groups found this was an assault on their personal behaviour and values.

2. using language that was excessively technical and concealed the main issues.

3. throwing up procedural blocks to prevent environmental groups from obtaining injunctions against companies to stop polluting. (254)

The application of these techniques in the context of public interest hearings seemed excessively technocratic and inappropriate and created an uncomfortable atmosphere in many hearings. (255) The impressions that many people formed is that lawyers, acting in collusion with administators as the hired guns for industry, often prevented local heroes from fighting for a clean environment or a just social cause.(256)

The problems which underlies this conflict is much deeper than this allusion reveals. The resentment that many feel stems in part from a perception that "grey-suited" bureaucrats and lawyers are often better equipped to deal with the EIA because they understand the procedural basis of the hearings and the policies which must be balanced and can argue the case for the option they advocate more effectively as a result. (257)

This suggests the structural dilemma that administrators face in providing intervenor funding. As noted already, members of the public frequently do not have the advocacy skills required to undertake cross examination of witnesses and prepare effective oral arguments. An alternative to hiring cousel would be to encourage the interested public and representatives of groups to develop advocacy skills. Several community groups offer seminars on advocacy skills and publish written materials to assist citizens and groups to make submissions before a board or tribunal. As noted above, this approach was adopted in the Beaufort EARP and appears to have proven fairly successful.

Despite the fact that people who speak before tribunals may not have much training, their message can often be more powerful when it is not mediated through lawyers. Experience with the Mackenzie Valley Pipeline Inquiry proved there is no reason why lawyers must "own the floor" during public hearings. Berger took this view in planning the Mackenzie Valley Pipeline Inquiry and the result was very effective. He established two tiers of participation; community-based hearings and formal hearings. At the community hearings, native people were encouraged to speak and few lawyers were present. In contrast, the formal hearings involved lawyers and regular techniques of cross-examination were employed. (258)

Berger's technique of dividing the hearings into two parts ensured that less money would have to be provided to groups and that the information provided was not filtered through political mechanisms. Inefficiencies of repetition were evident and it could be argued that this is generally not an appropriate way to encourage participation of up to a third or half the community. Over the past decade, the federal government has developed a modification of the Berger model in the North that minimizes the need for this kind of repetition. DIAND has taken the position that native groups must be funded to allow them to do community surveys, engage counsel, undertake travel, etc. so their leaders can make representative statements at hearings. Thus, the two-tier model that Berger devised has been elaborated considerably. Nevertheless, funding needs will generally be much smaller when this two-tier model is employed. As a matter of practice, the advantages to this style of funding are clear. It is noteworthy that this modified two-tier model was also employed in the Beaufort EARP.

1. Funding Mechanisms

Having now surveyed some of the factors that should be taken into account when designing an intervenor funding program, the different mechanisms available to government to support intervenor groups.

In his study for the Law Reform commission of Canada, David Fox (259) examines four methods of financing public interest interventions. Among these he includes the following:

1. Direct Grants From Government, Foundations and other Agencies;

2. A Check-off Levy system;

3. Cost Awards to Intervenors;

4. Loans to Intervenors.

Each of these methods will be examined herein with a view to an analysis of which would be most efficient and cost-effective in an era of fiscal restraint. In addition, other options outlined by Englehart and Trebilcock (260) such as tax credits will also be considered.

(a) Direct grants

The mechanism which has been used most frequently in Canada and the United States to fund intervenors is direct grants of money. The money is used towards various expenses including payment of counsel, experts and staff of interest groups, costs for preparation of documentation and other expenses. (261)

In an era of fiscal restraint it is clear that the relative merit of potential contributors must be evaluated. In order to facilitate this evaluation process, Berger developed the following five criteria to assess the validity of funding requests made by groups that wished to participate in the Mackenzie Valley Pipeline Inquiry hearings:

1. There should be a clearly ascertainable interest that ought to be represented at the Inquiry.

2. It should be clear that separate and adequate representation of that interest will make a necessary and substantial contribution to the Inquiry.

3. Those seeking funds should have an established record of concern for, and should have demonstrated their own commitment to, the interest they seek to represent.

4. It should be shown that those seeking funds do not

have sufficient financial resources to enable them
adequately to represent that interest, and will require
funds to do.

5. Those seeking funds should have a clear proposal as
to the use they intend to make of the funds, and should
be sufficiently well-organized to account for the funds.
(262)

This funding criteria was widely publicized and became a general
standard to measure potential needs of different groups for
funding in other inquiries which followed (263). In terms of the
Berger Inquiry, only 21. groups were deemed eligible,
representing everything from business groups to native mental
health workers. However, it is noteowrthy that neither the
Canadian Labour Congress or a Vancouver women's group were unable
to get money.

In total the Berger Inquiry made approximately $1.77 million
available for funding intervenors. This money was used towards a
variety of cost factors and the result of the funding program was
that provincial governments felt pressure to implement similar
programs for their environmental assessment procedures.

The first provincial goverenment in Canada to respond with
legislation to demands for intervenor funding of public
participation for an environmental assessment review that was
Saskatchewan. At the time public participation had become an
issue in the assessment of a large uranium mining proposal in
northern Saskatchewan. Under the relevant act, the Minister of
the Environment can grant persons or groups that are preparing or
presenting briefs up to $10,000. (264) However, some critics
claim that the Conservative government that was elected in 1983

in the province has all but rendered irrelevant the intent of this legislation by holding few inquiries and limitng access to funds.

(b) Access to Government Experts

Another way to support intervenor groups directly is to provide them with access to experts in government that can help with the review of complex submissions made by proponents. In Canada, this type of mechanism has not been used widely. One noteworthy exception is the Ontario statue which allows the responsible tribunal to make governement experts available to intervenor groups. (265)

Generally most intervenor groups do not support this alternative for fairly predicatble reasons. The biggest concern is that the government experts may not be willing to fully criticize other government officials or approach the issues "objectively". (266) Nevertheless, often intervenor groups have relied on leaked information and the support of sympathetic individuals in government agencies. Some of the best examples of this phenomena took place during the Berger Inquiry. In fact, many of the juiciest tidbits in Dosman's treatise were from leaked documents.(267)

The question then is whether this type of support is a realistic alternative to direct funding when money is scarce. Clearly, provisions which encourage consultation between interest groups and government could prove to be a relatively inexpensive means of support. However, the question remains: would it work?

Goodman has criticized this type of approach to citizen participation, based on his experiences in the 1960s with attempts to reform urban planning in New York city. (268) He argues that:

> within the present economic structure of our society, simply giving the poor more access to planning expertise doen't basically change their chances of getting the same goods and services as wealthier citizens. What it gives them is more power to compete among themselves for government's welfare products.(269)

Whether or not one agrees with Goodman, the general point that such a system cannot ultimately provide interest groups and other public interest intervenors with a measure of justice in our present socio-economic fabric is well-taken. Given the experience of environmental and native groups with agencies such as the AECB and federal departments like DIAND, it is unlikely that such an approach could work to support greater amounts of public participation in federal decision-making. Thus, I would not advocate this form of funding as a basis for a new federal program.

(C) Tax Credits

The basic idea for a tax credit has been outlined by Trebilcock and Englehart in an excellent article. (270) Using such a system a group would be able to get a tax credit depending on the number of members that belonged to their organization. This would allow a tribunal to disentitle a zealous group that was disrupting the hearing process.

One of the advantages of such a system would be that it would be easier to administer and remove elements of discretion from the funding process. In addition, Trebilcock and Englehart contend that a this system would foster "internal efficiency" because more effective groups will be able to use their money to undertake more representational efforts and allow the funded group to attract more members to their cause in the process.(271) The problem with the tax credit is that it would not work in the environmental area because the number of individual willing to join an environmental group never seems to reflect the requisite proportion of support that the group requires because most people are not adequately apprised of the true gravity of environmental problems today. In addition, these groups do not have the kind of cash flow that would be desirable in order to maximize the benefits of such a program.

(d) Check-Off Levy System

According to Fox (272), this system would allow specialized or individualized interventions. A group would send a donation request to members, consumers or subscribers. If the individual supported the particular initiative, then he or she could begin to contribute to the particular project or intervention.

The problem with this model is that it would not work for most environmental groups because they already have frequent mailings throughout the year requesting money and support form their membership. For those that make fewer requests, it is possible that such a model would work.

(e) Cost Awards

In terms of historical practice in Canada, cost awards have been the most popular means to fund and support public interest intervenors.(273) The reasons for this are quite simple. There is no doubt that cost awards make a great deal of sense for funding many intervenor groups and have proven efficient relative to other mechanisms, as Blue argues.(274) Consequently many tribunals in Canada have the power to award costs to public interest groups that make effective presentations and written submissions.

Over the past few years the power of the various tribunals in Canada with powers to award costs to environmental groups have generally adopted a conservative approach to costs. This trend has also been affirmed by many courts in Canada. The discussion above has already alluded to the recent decision in the <u>Bell Canada</u> case. (275) However, it also important to recognize that the <u>Bell Canada</u> case was preceded by two decisions of the Divisional Court in Ontario which also denied public interest groups cost awards.(276) One commentator has noted that, in the aggregate, these cases remind one of the "medieval perception that litigation was an evil disruption of the social order and therefore should be discouraged." (277)

In the result this experience does not suggest that cost awards are a suitable method for funding groups. The mechanism grants those in key positions an excessive amount of discretionary power to determine who will get costs, when, and how, and this seems to put most public interest intervenors in a difficult position.

(f) Loans

Another options that has been proposed is loans to intervenor groups for the duration of the Inquiry, requiring repayment afterwards.(278) This does not seem like a reasonable option in view of the points that have already been made about the funding situation facing public interest groups. Moreover, groups might be tempted to extend themselves if they thought they had an unlimited trough and this would probably worsen the financial stability of these groups over the long-term.

(g) Summary

Based on the discussion above it is apparent that the best mechanism for supporting public interest groups that participate in public hearings on environmental issues is direct funding. Experience suggests that environmental groups require funding "up front" in order to maximize their contribution to hearings and begin research well in advance of the actual hearings. Moreover, the other systems could potentially lead to the inappropriate exercize of discretion by government to exclude certain participants and might also produce inconsistencies over the long term. Over the long-term, a movement a tax credit system might be appropriate for reasons outlined above but, in the interim, the current system of direct grants should continue to be employed.

2. Some Modest Proposals

Having considered the arguments for and against direct funding and reviewed the experience with several inquiries in Canada, Britain and the United States it is now possible to make some general recommendations and propose workable guidelines for determining who to fund and when to fund them. This discussion assumes that the availability of funds will be restricted for fiscal reasons and it is necessary to limit the number of groups that participate both for cost reasons related to the hearing as well as the scarcity of funds for intervenors generally.

(a) General Recommendations

Prior to proposing workable guidelines and criteria for selecting eligible groups for intervenor funding it is necessary to briefly review the key features of the participation process and draw some conclusions.

As a point of departure it must be reiterated that not all government policies and major projects require either public funding to ensure a wide range of views are represented or merit detailed attention. Moreover, it must be admitted that it is difficult to establish workable criteria for intervenor funding in many cases because decision-makers must first consider some "meta-level" questions about the nature of public participation. The answers to these questions, some of which are outlined below and discussed briefly, will determine the nature and extent of the funding needs of participants.

1. Should public participation be regular and continuous?

Continuity of involvement is often important because it allows certain groups to develop skills and learn the decision-making process. Without continuity, funding can yield haphazard results and undermine the credibility of efforts to involve the public.

2. Should public participation be pro-active or merely re-active to policy-making and planning?

As Emond contends, there is a strong argument to be made for pro-active public participation in environmental planning. (279) However, most agencies are reluctant to engage in pro-active planning. The Beaufort EARP was an important exception which demonstrates the value of this approach.

3. Should the communication be two-way or one-way?

As the discussion above suggested, there is always a danger that communication may become one-way, rather than uni-dimensional. Moreover, legitimization of public participation will require that communication be two-way, particularly when class issues arise. In the Berger Inquiry, this was amply apparent. Berger undertook genuine dialogue with the communities and carefully listened to the concerns of the native people. Other inquiries often have relied on more conventional, tokenistic mechanisms(280), reminding one of Habermas's argument that this type of adaptation does not address the structural source of domination small communities may feel when confronted with a large development proposal. (281)

4. What range of issues and concerns should be addressed?

In certain inquiries or decisions, the discussion may touch on local, regional provincial and federal responsibilities. Ultimately it may be necesary to earmark funding to groups on the premise that they will direct their attentions to issues relating to one or two responsibilities. For example, Beaufort hearings were divided in such a way that federal matters were commented on by interest groups with a national scope such as the BSA while regional and local matters were left to the local communities.

5. Should interest groups be encouraged to research and comment on matters that might otherwise appear outside of their area of expertise?

In complex decisions there is an argument for an interdisciplinar approach. For example, often considerable overlap exists between social and environmental impacts as experience with the EARP shows. It may be difficult to seperate the two different kinds of input which would tend to suggest that divisions such as that outlined in discussion of Question 4 above may be arbitrary.

These are only some of the meta-level questions about participation that must be addressed prior to initiating a funding program. In addition, it will be necessary to consider further criteria for selecting groups once the initial decision is made.

(b) Guidelnes for Determining Who to Fund

The experiences outlined above suggest that the choice of who to fund has an important bearing on the contributions made by intervenors groups to regulatory and decision-making processes. In view of the various schemes that have been employed in the past and the considerations that have been outlined in the analysis above, I would jsuggest the following variables should be taken into account in future decisions on intervenor funding:

1. Complexity of the Decision. Certain decisions merit more involvement than others because they have synergistic impacts.

2. Social Vulnerability of the Group Represented. Experience with the Beaufort and Berger Inquiries shows that public support exists for funding groups representing constituencies with low social mobility, such as northern native peoples. It could be argued that similar types of groups such as farmers should also recieve special help

3. Fund-raising Capability. This relates to the fourth criterion applied by Berger. It should be noted that some community groups can draw extensively on local individuals to help with fund-raising if they are given sufficient time to do so.

4. Group Origin. Self-generated groups which arise to protest decisions that have significant differential impacts on local populations may have a greater need than those associated with business interests or local unions.

5. Geographical Factors. Groups or citizens that are close to urban centres or universities may have access to low-cost consultants, university professors or graduate students to help with basic research and writing . Conversely, geographical isolation may force a group to incur high travel costs to those centres and enormous telephone bills.

6. Type of Interest Involved. The funded group should represent an identifiable interest which will make a significant contribution to the rule-making or decision-taking process.

7. Uniqueness of Interest. A public interest group
may meet criterion 6 but the interest may also be well
represented by other groups. Consequently there is a
need to assess whether funding should be provided
in order to obtain another assessment of the policy
or the project. It should be noted here that care
must be exercized in the application of this
criterion.

8. Historical commitment to the Issue(s). As the
discussion of problems with EIA showed, public
intervenors have a tendency to lose interest during
long and tedioius procedures that may be involved with
the preparation of impact statements. Groups and
citizens with demonstrated commitment to an issue
are likely to remain involved in longer hearings.

9. Planned Use of Funds. Groups with an indigenous
research capacity may well be able to draw on their
regular staff to prepare reports or make oral
presentations. similarly, other groups may not possess
this type of capacity and limited funds provided
to this latter groups will yield inadequte
representation.

The significance of these criteria will vary depending on the
type of issue under consideration. For example, the experience
of the Berger Inquiry and other northern inquiries suggests large
amount of money should be provided when the issues to be
considered are complex and require consideration of both physical
and social impacts. (282)

Similarly this critera could also be strategically employed
to reduce costs. For example, in the Beaufort EARP the Funding
Committee structured participation to reduce the amount of travel
required by participants. Thus, hearings were held in Calgary
and Ottawa for southern oil industry officials, government
officials and interest groups. In contrast, those held in
Yellowknife and Inuvik considered the concerns of northern groups
and communities primarily.

There are also limits to this kind of framework. For example, Exclusivity of the interest at stake may be a poor guide for funding in many cases. Clearly, there is an argument for "overlapping research data interpretation. Not only do groups approach problems from different viewpoints, they will reflect their values and attitudes in quite different ways and should be encouraged to do so if these viewpoint are legitimate and they meet the other critera outlined here. In order to to this it might be necessary to provide less per capita support for each group or encourage these groups to coordinate a certain amount of basic research.

The question as to how widely intervenor groups should be allowed to stray in their presentations is not a simplistic one either. For example, often the vocal criticisms of one group can bring into focus a matter deserving of public attention and force the government to implement new policies or legisltion. Certainly this appears to have been one consequence of the efforts of Pollution Probe roundly criticized existing federal environmental protection laws in their initial submissions to the Berger Inquiry. (284)

One of the crucial factos that must be considered in any attempt to increase public participation in decision-making is the structure of the modern industrial state. As Galbraith (285) has argued in his classic treatment of the subject, concentrations of interests which are closely aligned with government often have inordinate amounts of power in democratic political systems. The mechanisms behind the alignement process and actual perpetuation of corporate power are extremely complex and cannot be explored here in any detail. Suffice to note that the connections between government and industrial power brokers often became apparent through confliect of interst scandals (286). Moreover, previous experience shows that public interst groups have often been able to show these connections through attacks on the credibility and indpendence cf individuals appointed to tribunals by government. An example of this was provided during the NEB hearings for the Mackenzie Valley Pipeline when a former chairman of Canadian Arctic Gas, Marshall Crowe, was appointed as Chairman of the tribunal. This appointment outraged certain groups and it was successfully challenged by the interest groups who argued that it was a blatant example of bias in administrative proceeding. Ironically, one could probably trace some of the money used to pay for the court costs in this case to funds donated to the public interest groups involved during the Berger Inquiry.

(c) When to Fund

In addition to the matter of selecting which groups to fund, it is also necessary to deal with the matter of when to fund them. Conceptually it is difficult to separate the question of timing from the question of selection of appropriate groups to fund. Different groups will have different contributions to make at various stages in project decisions or policy-making. For example, a wilderness conservation group may have a valid opinion on a development project in an exceptional area and early contact between the group and a proponent may allow the two parties to work out compromises. (283) However, that same group may not have a clear interest that merits attention when the issue of day care facilities for the project is dealt with at a later stage in the hearings. Thus funding them for hearings on the latter issue might be inappropriate and costly.

Conclusion

In his book Electronic Nightmare, John Wicklein offers two possible scenarios that the new communications technologies can encourage in the industrialized West. (287) He identifies these as authoritarian centalization and democratic decentralization. Regarding the former, he contends that new communications technologies make possible a system in which government can extract all the information it needs to control the lives of its citizenry and transmit the information to those tht would be responsible for controlling them.

No doubt some academics and social critics feared the kind of Orwellion scenario which would emerge if the growth of public consultation and education had continued unabated through the 1950s. It was these people who began to advocate democratization of the electronic media because

> [i]t also makes possible a system in which authority can spread across an enlightened populace. In this second model, communication is multilateral -- two-way between government and people, and among the people themselves. Through it a vast diversity of information could be disseminated to give people the knowledge they need to govern their own lives effectively and make infcrmed decisions about local and national policies. (288)

Not surprisingly, CARC has roundly criticized the application of this type of advertising in the context of northern development as misleading and inappropriate. (290)

Nevertheless, it is doubtful that industry will relent on their commitment to advocacy advertising and this suggests a need for greater regulation of the media. If this approach is not supported then it will become imperative for the governments in Canada to increase intervenor funding in all spheres of public life, if only to give the appearance of justice and fair hearing to different viewpoints in policy-making.

In the context of environmental decision-making, it is unclear what the future holds. If Canada is a leader in impact assessment today, it is due in part to the efforts of sensitive lawyers and administrators who have attempted over the last decade to integrate the best features of administrative law into the EIA decision-making process. Accordingly, principles of natural justice (such as the right to adequate notice and an oral hearing) have guided their efforts and greatly expanded the importance of public participation and consultation in public decision-making. But as important in this overall reform thrust has been the expansion of other support mechanisms such as intervenor funding. The continued development of these support mechanisms should be encouraged in the environmental assessment field and perhaps extended to other aspects of regulation. There are some positive signs that this indeed is taking place. But there are others which could suggest many of the programs that were implemented over the last decade may be curtailed due to fiscal restraint.

This would indeed be a tragedy. Increased participation in environment decision-making has served to revitalize participation in other spheres of government activity as well. Federal environmental inquiries have provided numerous groups with experience and confidence for participation in other inquiries and commissions on a broad range of issues and matters. In fact, many of the goups who interveded at the Berger Inquiry and other northern inquiries contributed significantly to the recent Macdonald Commission. (291) Through their experiences with public hearings, these groups have begun to realize they have a valid contribution to make to government decision-making. Particularly intriguing are the efforts made by church groups. Their criticisms of government policy have become much more vocal recently. While it would be inaccurate to state that the publication of This Land is Not for Sale (292) by the McCullums, who were key figures in the United Church at the time (1975), was a turning point in this process of involvement it did signal an important breakthrough. After this book was distributed an allegiance between the United Church and native people grew and the other churches began to join in their fight to have land claims settled prior to construction of the Mackenzie Valley Pipeline. In the recent past this activism has expanded into numerous other spheres as well, and served to highlight the deep structural tensions emerging in the Canadian State.

Whatever the fate of intervenor funding in the future, we can learn something about the law reform process through analysis of the Berger Inquiry. No doubt the spread of support throughout Canada for increased public participation after the Inquiry confirms that an important precedent will open the floodgates and allow many people to access to decision-makers on panels and tribunals. Berger, in opening the floodgates for native people and environmental groups in the north, guaranteed that subsequent groups would have the visible precedent they needed to continue the experiment he began with intervenor funding. The fact that the Berger Inquiry still is cited in literature on intervenor funding throughout the world suggests its long-term significant decision-making in modern industrial nations.

This episode in Canadian history also shows support for the contention that the New Democratic Party has had an important effect on legal reforms in Canada.(293) If the NDP had not pressured the Liberal Minority government to fund intervenor groups for participation in the Berger Inquiry, it is doubtful that broad public support for the policy could have been achieved as rapidly in Canada. The fact that other nations are now implementing the World Conservation Strategy as a basis for environmental decision-making suggests that the reform will have global significance in the long-term. Perhaps the major consolation of this innovation is that it is one of the few examples of an appropriate technology exported from Canada to the Third World. Hopefully it is one we will remain proud of for decades.

NOTES

1. C. Swayze, Hard Choices: A Life of Tom Berger (1987). Vancouver: Douglas and McIntyne.

2. The Inquiry report is contained in two volumes: T. R. Berger, Northern Frontier, Northern Homeland: The Report of the Mackenzie Valley Pipeline Inquiry, 2 vols. (1977). Toronto: James Lorimer. Hereinafter: Berger, Inquiry. One of the best introductions to the politics of the Berger Inquiry is F. Bregha, "A Ten Year Muddle: The Northern Pipeline and Canadian Energy Policy" (1979-80), Canadian Forum (December 1979-January 1980). For a summary description of the Berger Inquiry as a process of decision-making, see D. Gamble, "The Berger Inquiry: An Impact Assessment Process," (1978) 199 Science 946. Background material on Berger's efforts to secure intervenor funding for the Inquiry and a thorough survey of many aspects of northern development in Canada may be found in R. Page, Northern Development: The Canadian Dilemma (1986). Toronto: McClelland and Stewart. Hereinafter: Page, Northern Development.

3. Swayze, Hard Choices, supra note 1 at pp.

3a. Page, ibid, pp. 90-91.

3b. For a summary of the arguments and ideas on the influence of developments in administrative law and their impact on public participation, see A. Roman, "Recent Developments in the 'Right' to Participate" (1984) in N. Bankes and J. Owen Saunders (eds.) Public Disposition of Natural Resources. Essays from the First Banff Conference on Natural Resources Law, Banff, Alberta, April 12-15, 1983. Calgary: Canadian Institute of Resources Law (CIRL).

4. B. Fox, "The High Price of Winning", Toronto Star, February 27, 1982, p. B5. Fox points out that the federal government provided $1 million to native groups to fight the new Constitution and undertake legal actions in the British courts.

5. For the purposes of this paper, "public participation" refers to the various levels of community involvement that individual citizens and public interest groups may pursue depending on options available to them. For discussion, see infra at pp.

6. Barry B. Boyer, "Funding Public Participation in Agency Proceedings: The Federal Trade Commission Experience" (1981), The Georgetown Law Journal 40. See also, B. Checkoway, "The Politics of Public Hearings" (1981), 17(4) Journal of Applied Behavioural Science.

7. See Rudy Platiel, "Ontario Cabinet overturns ruling by OMB against citizens group", The Globe and Mail, February 17, 1987, P. A14. For a comment on the decision and an argument for funding, see S. Shrybman, "The Modest Cost of Public

8. The most important recent Supreme Court of Canada decision is Bell Canada v. Consumers Association of Canada (1986), 17 Admin. L.R. 205 (S.C.C.). In this case, Ledain J. held that public participation is an important part of regulatory decision-making but that in this case the Canadian Radio and Television Commission's taxing officer was entitled to consider the funding arrangements of the groups involved before awarding costs. For a review of this case and other important recent decisions on intervenor funding, see J. Evans, ... (1987), Supreme Court L. R. (full cite please)

9. The leading Canadian article on the question of intervenor funding in environmental decision-making is R. Anand and I. Scott, "Financing Public Participation in Environmental Decision-Making", (1982) 60 Can. Bar Rev. 82. It is noteworthy that Ian Scott, one of the co-authors of the article, was Commission Counsel to the Berger Inquiry, discussed infra at pp. . As I point out later this inquiry was a turning point in the development of federal policies on intervenor funding. This may explain why Scott felt obliged to provide funding to the citizen group that intervened to the OMB on agricultural land conservation as mentioned in note 7. A great deal of other recent articles in the area of intervenor funding in Canada has been generated by individuals associated with the Canadian Environmental Law Association (CELA). CELA has done considerable lobbying for awarding of costs for environmental groups that intervene on behalf of the public. For a background document, see F. Giorno, " A Brief to Ontario's Mininster of the Environment on Intervenor Funding" (1984). Prepared for the Canadian Environmental Law Association on behalf of the Citizens Network Concerned about Waste Management. Girono, Director of Research for CELA, contends that the brief put pressure on the Ontario Cabinet to provide funding to groups reviewing plans for the Ontario Waste Management Corporations facilities. See discussion, infra pp.

10. For a critical overview on the emergence of the modern industrial state, see R. Goodman, After the Planners. (1971). New York: Simon and Schuster.

11. The leading summary of the contribution of these thinkers to liberal democractic perceptions on public participation is C. B. MacPherson, The Life and Times of Liberal Democracy (1977). Toronto: Macmillan.

12. See E. P. Thompson's description of "rough music" as a technique for enforcing local justice in Whigs and Hunters (1975). Extracted in D. Hay (ed.) Materials and Readings for Law and Social Change (1986). Downsview: Osgoode Hall Law School, York University.

13. John Hogarth, "Status to Contract: The Legalization of Attitudes and Relationships", in D. Gibson and J. K. Baldwin (eds.) Law in a Cynical Society? Opinion and Law in the 1980's (1985). Calgary: Carswell Legal Publications; pp. 327-333.

14. G. E. Mingay, The Gentry: The Rise and Fall of the Ruling Class (1976). London: Longman.

15. H. Arthurs, Without the Law. (1985). Toronto: University of Toronto Press.

16. P. Bachrach, The Theory of Democractic Elitism (1967). Boston: Litle, Brown and Company.

17. C. Pateman, Participation and Democratic Theory (1970). London: Cambridge University Press.

18. J. Schumpeter, Capitalism, Socialism and Democracy (1942). New York: Harper and Row.

19. Ibid, pp.

20. Bachrach, supra note 16.

21. In Canada one of the most notorious examples of this form of elite participation took place in the development of nuclear power. The AECB required baseline studies and assessments from the very outset in the 1950s. However, once facilities were completed public hearings were not held. Instead, local information offices were opened and selected persons such as doctors were invited to take one-week courses in nuclear energy and radiological health. For further discussion, see P. Mckay, Electric Empire (1984). Toronto: Between-the-Lines Press.

22. R. R. Alford, Bureaucracy and Participation (1969). Chicago: Rand MacNally and Co; p. 77. Alford relates this process to the broader process of secularization as well: "Bureaucratization is related to the development of secularization, the freeing of men from traditional ties of kin and tribe which prevents them from rationally adjusting means to ends."

23. For background on this matter, see E. Belobaba, Jack Berkow et al., On the Question of Consumer Advocacy -- A Working Paper (1972). Ottawa: Canadian Consumer Council. The Consumer Council commissioned this study to recommend reforms for regulatory agencies. Noteworthy are five recommendations made for improving consumer representation in the regulatory process.

24. Paul Wilkinson, Public Participation and Environmental Management" Unpublished Ph.D. Thesis, University of Toronto, 1974, p. 26.

25. Ibid, p. 26

26. Ibid, p. 30

27. Background on this is provided by W. Leiss, The Limits to Satisfaction (1976). Toronto: University of Toronto Press.

28. B. Doern, "Megaprojects in Canada", (1984) <u>Canadian Public Administration</u>.

29. T. Schrecker, <u>The Political Economy of Environmental Hazards</u> (1984). A Study Paper Prepared for the Law Reform Commission of Canada. Ottawa: Ministry of Supply and Services.

30. <u>Mckie</u> v. <u>K.V.P. Co. Ltd.</u>, [1948] 3 D.L.R. 201 (O.H.C.J.) per McRuer C.J.H.L.

31. A. Shkilnyk, <u>A Poison Stronger than Love: The Destruction of an Ojibwa Community</u> (1985). New Haven: Yale University Press.

32. For a description of Swedish experiments to public participation in the 1960s and 1970s, see Soren Haggroth "Public Participation in the Design and Management of the Residential Environment" in <u>Swedish Experiences of Self-Building, Cooperation Consumer Research and Participation</u> (1976). Stockholm: Ministry of Housing and Physical Planning. This was Sweden's contribution to the United Nations Conference on Human Settlements, HABITAT, in Vancouver, 1976.

33. M. Janowitz, <u>The Last Half Century: Social Change and Politics in America</u> (1978). Chicago: University of Chicago Press; pp. 270-271.

34. Milton Kotler, <u>Neighborhood Government: The Local Foundation of Political Life</u> (1969). New York: The Bobbs Merrill Co.

35. For background on this, see Pateman, <u>Participation and Democratic Theory supra</u>, note 17. Pateman, an Australian professor now, was moved to write this book by the student movements of the 1960s. The book "bubbles over" with optimism about the possibility for greater public involvement in decision-making. Her views have since been tempered by failed experiments, as her more recent book, <u>The Problem of Political Obligation</u> (1979). New York: J. Wiley and Sons, shows.

36. Amitai Etzioni, "Towards a Theory of Societal Guidance" (1967), 73(2) <u>American Jour. of Sociology</u> 173

37. Modified from Lucas and McCallum, <u>infra</u> note

38. Orion F. White Jr., "The Dialectical Organization: An Alternative to Brureaucracy" (1969), <u>Public Administration Review</u> 32

39. See G. Inglis, "Giving Community Development Back to the People" (1975), <u>Canadian Welfare</u> (Jan-Feb. 1975)

40. D. W. R. Sewell and J. T. Coppock, <u>Public Participation in Planning</u> (1977). New York: John Wiley and Sons. This book

provides a useful overview of early Canadian experience with public participation in planning in Canada.

41. Herbert G. Wilcox, "Hierarchy, Human Native and the Participative Panacea" (1969), Public Administration Review 53

42. J. O'Riordan and T. O'Riordan, "How Can Citizen Input Best be Utilized by Decision-Makers," in B. Sadler (ed.) Natural Workshop on Public Participation in Environmental Decision-Making (1980). Based on Conference, Banff, Alberta, April 17-20, 1979.

43. J. Simmie, Citizens in Conflict (1975). London: Hutichinson.

44. For introductory articles on this, see Henry C. Hart, "Crisis, Community and Consent in Water Politics" (1973), 57 Law and Contemporary Problems 510, R. E. Kasperson, "Political Behaviour and the Decision-Making Process in the Allocation of Water Resources and Between Recreational and Municipal Use" (1969), 9 Natural Resources Journal 176

45. See, B. H. Dodge "Achieving Public Involvment in the Corps of Engineers Water Resources Planning" (****), 9(3) Water Resources Bulletin 448. Several essays in the book, L. B. Dworsky, D. J. Allee and S. C. Csallary (eds.). National Symposium on Social and Economic Aspects of Water Resources Development (1972). Ithaca: American Water Resources Association, are also helpful.

46. On the problem of boundary definition in relation to water management, see Charles F. Warriner, "Public Opinion and Collective Action: Formation of a Watershed District" (1978), 6(3) Administrative Science Quarterly 333.

47. An excellent example of this type of frustration was provided in a public review of alternatives for a project on the Grand River in Southwestern Ontario. In a letter to the Minister of the Environment, Carl Ott wrote the following:

> It seems to me to be a very undemocratic situation when a group opposed to a proposal of such a far reaching significance has to struggle against almost unsurmountable odds and go into personal debt, while the government hands out another large sum of taxpayer's money to an organization that already spent hundreds of thousands of dollars in their attempt to justify the building of the dam.

Printed in Ontario Ministry of the Environment Grand River Basin Water Management Study, Technical Report No. 21 (1977); pp. 104-106.

48. James K. Thompson, "The Developing Art of Decision-Making for a People-Oriented Society" in S. Bendix and H. R. Graham (eds.) Environmental Assessment: Approaching Maturity (1978).

Ann Arbour, Michigan: Ann Arbour Science Publishers Inc.

49. D. Torgerson, "From Dream to Nightmare: The Historical Origin's of Canada's Nuclear Electric Future" (1977), 7(1) Alternatives: Perspectives on Society and Environment.

50. B. Doern, supra note 28.

51. For other similar examples in the water resource area, see J. L. Creighton (ed.) Public Involvement Techniques: A Reader on Ten Years' Experience at the Institute for Water Resources (1982). Belvoir, Virginia: U.S. Army Corps of Engineers.

52. It is essential to keep in mind the fact that the Port Hope community had been sensitized to the issue of nuclear waste disposal in the mid 1970s. In July 1975 a representative of Energy Probe, a group that split-off from Pollution Probe earlier that year, had called for an investigation into the high levels of radioactivity in the Port Hope area on a CBC Program. In response, Donald McDonald, Energy Minister for the federal government at the time had ordered an investigation by the AECB. The subsequent report showed that Eldorado Nuclear Ltd. had been lax in its management of nuclear wastes. As a result over 100 locations in the town of Port Hope were found to have been contaminated with radioactivity. This provided grassroots concern and motivated considerable interest in the further work of both Eldorado and the AECB. For further discussion, see P. Sanger, Blind Faith: The Nuclear Industry in One Small Town (1981). Toronto: McGraw-Hill.

53. An outline of the application of different models of public participaton to water resources managment in the United States is presented in A. C. Davis, J. Anderson and R. Gough Alternative Information and Interaction Approaches to Public Participation in Water Resources Decision-Making (1975). Water Resources Research Institute of the University of North Carolina.

54. For a survey, see D. Vindains, Public Participation Techniques and Methodologies: A Resume (1974). Ottawa: Information Canada. See also D. M. Connor, "Models and Techniques of Citizen Participation" (1977), 1 Involvement and Environment

55. A classic argument for public participation in environmental decision-making is David L. Thomsen, Public Participation in Water and Land Managment (1973). Ithaca, New York: Cornell. While the analysis focuses primarily on the experiences in water management, the general rules are applicable in most areas of environmental management.

56. Ibid.

57. P. McKay, supra note 21.

58. M. O. Ertel, "Identification of Training Needs for Public

Participation Responsibilities" (****), 16(2) Water Resources
Bulletin 300

59. For a Canadian perspective on ths problem, see P. C.
Vrooman, "The Power Dilemma in Citizen Participation" (1972)
Canadian Welfare (May-June 1972). Note that this magazine is now
called Perception.

60. James A. Riedel, "Citizen Participation: Myths and
Realities" (1972), 32 Public Administration Review 211.

61. H. Buchbinder, G. Hunnius and E. Stevens. Citizen
Participation: A Research Framework and Annotated Bibliography
(1974). Ottawa: Ministry of Urban Affairs.

62. Thomsen, supra note 55. See also the essays in A. Utton
(ed.) Natural Resources for a Democratic Society: Public
Participation in Decision-Making (1977). Boulder, Colorado:
Westview.

63. On this argument about public pariciption as an alternaive
to anarchic rebellion, see Geraint Parry, "Orderly and Disorderly
Conduct: Some Recent Work on Political Participation" (****),
15(2) Government and Opposition 223.

64. Boris Komarov, The Destruction of Nature in the Soviet Union
(1980). White Plains, New York: M. E. Sharpe. See especially
comments at p. 138.

65. Tony Barber, "Soviets scrap controversial river plans", The
Globe and Mail, August 26, 1986, p. A10.

66. For background on the Stockholm Conference and its impact on
environmental policy-making and public participation, see P.
Stone, "Stockholm Revisited" (1982), 1 Uniterra 2. A general
exposition on the Conference is W. Rowland, The Plot to Save the
World: The Stockholm Conference on the Human Environment (1973).
Toronto: Macmillan.

71. Soon after the Stockholm Conference, the United Nations
Environmental Protection (UNEP) agency was established. This
agency has sponsored numerous conferences on environmental
issues. Moreover, UNEP formed a coalition with the International
Union for the Conservation of Nature and Natural Resources (IUCN)
(and was later joined by the World Wildlife Fund) to sponsor the
World Conservation Strategy. This has been the focal point for
numerous conservation conferences for the past four or five
years. In addition UNEP sponsored a study on Environment and
Development that toured most industrial nations in 1985 and 1986.
For background, see D. McRobert, "Canada and the World
Conservation Strateghy (1986), 9(1) Probe Post 31. It should be
stressed that all these processes have involved substantial
amounts of public participation but no funding was provided. In
view of some critics, these fora have merely acted as a vent for
frustrated environmentalists and drained energy and resources

from groups that might otherwise have invested their energies in law reform or raising consciousness.

72. Geoffrey Wandesforde-Smith, "The Bureaucratic Response to Environmental Politics" (1971), 11 Natural Resources Journal 479.

73. This experience served to build linkages between the groups. Consequently often leaks were made (always inexplicably) by former activists to their friends in environmental groups. This phenomena takes place in all government activities but is especially prevalent in the environmetal area. For a review of these developments and a survey of programs of Canadian Universities, see W. J. Couch and B. Rigby (eds) Environmental Assessment in Canada: Directory of University Training and Research, 1983-84 (1984). Ottawa: FEARO.

74. A survey of the contribution of these figures and a review of factors that contributed to the emergence of the environmental movement in the United States and Britain is found in T. O'Riordan, Environmentalism (1976). London: Pion.

75. U. S. Council on Environmental Quality, Regulations for Implementing the Procedural Provisions of the National Environmental Policy Act (1978). Washington, D. C.: U.S.G.P.O. Reprinted in 43 F.R. 55978-566007. For background and a description of the process, see Paul A. Erickson, Environmental Impact Assessment: Principles and Applications (1979). New York: Academic Press.

76. C. S. Holling, Adaptive Environmental Assessment and Management (1978). Chichester: J. Wiley and Sons.

77. D. Nelkin, "Public Participation in Environmental Planning in the U.S.A." in Y. Ahamad and G. G. Muller (eds.), Integrated Physical, Socio-Economic and Environmental Planning (1982). Dublin: Tycooly International Publishing Ltd.

78. E. Richardson, Dams, Parks and Politics: Resource Development in the Truman-Eisenshower Era (1973). Kentucky: University of Kentucky Press.

80. The intent behind the establishment of EIA was to democratize cost-benefit analysis which had become a paradigm example of technological rationality gone mad according to critics. As a method, EIA is much more political than CBA; the latter relies extensively on estimates made by economists about the value of goods and services while the former technique requires the public to assess the relative importance of environmental amenities when compared to other factors such as employment. For a classic description of cost-benefit analysis, see E. J. Mishan, Cost-Benefit Analysis, 2nd Ed. (1976). New York Praeger Press. Critiques of the application of cost benefit analysis have been widely published over the past two decades. An accessible introduction is P. Self, Econocrats and the Policy Process: The Politics and Philosophy of Cost-Benefit Analysis

(1975). London: Macmillan Press.

81. A. Armour, "Understanding Environmental Assessment," (1977) Plan Canada 8.

81a. It has been argued that the environmental movement acted as a surrogate for the widespread protest movement that had emerged in the United States during the Vietnam War. Politically, pollution was a motherhood issue and less threatening to the state than the other forms of protest that were gaining popularity at the time. Thus, most industrial nations were willing to respond to calls for reform through implementation of limited and primarily cosmetic measures that addressed visible problems such as air and water pollution. However, deeper problems such as acid rain and toxic pollution were not addressed and this may explain why the current situation has developed into a serious crisis in the eyes of some environmental thinkers. A heart-wrenching exposition on the failure of the environmental movement is J. Livingston, The Fallacy of Wildife Conservation (1981). Toronto: McCelland and Stewart.

82. See NEPA, section 102(2) (c), supra note 67.

83. K. F. Maurer, Public Participation in Environmental Assessment Hearings: An Analysis of Current Practice in Canada and the United States with Proposed Options for the Ontario Environmental Assessment Board. (1979). Toronto: Institute for Environmental Studies, University of Toronto.

84. On this point, see G. C. Gallopin Planning Methods and the Human Environment (1981). Paris: United Nations Education, Scientific and Cultural Organizations (UNESCO). As Gallopin observes, "the scarcer and more partial the factual knowledge about the system (as is essentially the case with the environment), the more likely is that the gaps of knowledge will be filled by the dominant preconceptions" (at p. 56).

85. F. Rossini, A. L. Porter, P. Kelly and D. E. Chubin, "Interdisciplinary Integration within Technology Assessments." (1981), 2(4) Knowledge 503

86. The classic critique of the problem of valuation of impacts in EIA is R. Bissett, "Quantification, Decision-Making and Environmental Impact Assessment in the United Kingdom" (1978), 7 J. Env. Managment 43. See also D. Schindler,

87. On the interaction between CBA and spiritual values, the most powerful argument for preserving the "non-economic" is Schumacher, Small is Beautiful (1975). New York: Abacus. At p. 41, Schumacher argues that in CBA

> Everything is equated with everything else. To equate things means to give them a price and thus make them exchangeable. to the extent that economic

> thinking is based on the market, it takes the
> sacredness out of life, because there can be nothing
> sacred in something that has a price. Not
> surprisingly, therefore, if economic thinking pervades
> the whole of society, even simple non-economic values
> like beauty, health or cleanliness can survive only if
> they prove economic.

If the federal government had relied on the estimates for the value of "country food' (e.g. wild meat and fish) eaten by native people along with the Mackenzie Valley Pipeline corridor offered by government and industry, they would have emulated this calculus. The original estimates did not properly account for either the nutritional or psychic value of this food and, as a result, did not accurately reflect the well-being of those living in the corridor. For further discussion on this, see Berger, Inquiry, supra note 2.

88. E. Bardach and L. Pugliaresi, "The Environmental Impact Statement v. The Real World" (1977). The Public Interest 22. At p. 29 the authors comment on the tendency for proponents to opt for comprehnsive surveys of impacts: "genuine and serious environmental problems are sufficiently numerous without crowding the political agenda with imagined ones as well ...."

89. U. S. Council on Environmental Quality. Scoping Guidance (1981). Washington, D. C.

90. Alan L. Porter et al. (eds) A Guidebook for Technology Assessment and Impact Analysis (1980). New York: North Holland Press. Hereinafter: Porter, Guidebook.

91. F. Curtis, "A Checklist for Writing and Presentation of Environmental Assessment Reports," (1982). 26(1) Canadian Geographer 64.

92. Government of Ontario, Ministry of the Environment, General Guidelines for the Preparation of Environmental Assessements (1978). Toronto: Ministry of the Environment.

93. H. M. Ingram, "Information Channels and Environmental Decison-Making" (1973) 13 Natural Resources Journal 150; H. Frauenglass, "Environmetal Policy: Public Participation and the Open Information System" (1971), 13 Natural Resources Journal 150. On the issue of timing and public disclosure, see David Estrin and John Swaigen, Environment on Trial (1978). Toronto: Canadian Environmental Law Research Foundation. Estrin and Swaigen note that constraints in scheduling may render badly-timed information useless. This speaks to the need for funding well in advance of the hearing process: see discussion, infra pp.

94. In support of this contention, see K. Rea, The Prosperous Years: The Economic History of Ontario, 1939-1975 (1985). Toronto: University of Toronto Press.

95. B. Woodrow, "Resources and Environmental Policy-Making at the National Level: The Search for Focus" in O.P. Dwivedi (ed.) Resources and the Environment: Policy Perspectives for Canada (1980). Tontonto: McClelland and Stewart.

95a. R. Lang and A. Armour, "The Process of Environmental Impact Assessment: Making it work for Canada" in Environmental Impact Assessment in Canada: Processes and Approaches (1977). Toronto: Institute of Environmental Studies, University of Toronto.

96. M. J. Trebilcock, "Regulators and the Consumer Interest: The Canadian Transport Commission's Cost Decision" (1977), 2 Can. Bus. L. J. 101. This is an important comment on a decision made by the CTC not to award costs to intervenors as a matter of principle. Over eighteen aspects of the decision are criticized and in the process Trebilcock inventories arguments for and against public participation in regulatory proceeding.

97. Regulated Industries Program, Consumer's Association of Canada, Cost Awards in Regulatory Proceedings: A Manual for Public Participants (1979). Ottawa: CAC.

98. See D. P. Emond, "Participation and the Environment: A Strategy for Democratizing Canada's Environmental Protection", (1975), 13 O.H.L.J. 783. Emond analyses laws that existed at the time and argues for a reform strategy based on a model that maximizes timely public participation.

98a. W.J. Baumol and W.E. Oates, Economics, Environmental Policy and the Quality of Life (1979). Englewood Cliffs, N.J.: Prentice-Hall.

99. Paul Lantz, "Costs as a Regulatory Device" (1981), 3 Advocates' Quarterly 396.

100. The Anglo -Canadian cost rule is that the "loser" pays most of the costs. In practice this rule is usually modified to suit particular circumstances by the Canadian courts. In the American system, each litigant pays his or her own costs. For discussion, see Lantz, ibid.

101. J. F. Castrilli, and J. Swaigen, "The American or the Canadian Costs Rule? An Empty Choice for the Public Interest Litigant" (1975), 4 C.E.L.N. 175. Generally, see also S. K. McCallum and G. Watkins, "Citizens' Costs Before Administrative Tribunals" (1975), 23 Chitty's L. J. 181.

102. Baumol and Oates, supra note 98a.

103. CAC, Cost Awards, supra note 97. For further background on this point in the context of environmental tribunals in Ontario, see Toby Vigod, "The Awarding of Costs by Environmental Boards" (1985). In Shelly Howwell (ed.), How to Fight For What's Left. Documents prepared for a One-Day Workshop sponsored by CELA,

February 22, 1985.

104. CAC, Cost Awards, Ibid.

105. R. Presthus, "Interest Groups and the Canadian Parliament: Activities, Interaction, Legitimacy and Influence" in Susan Didjanski (ed) Political Decision-Making Process (****).

106. On this point, see M. Bucovetsky "The Mining Industry and the Great Tax Reform Debate" in A. P. Pross (ed) Pressure Group Behaviour in Canadian Politics (1975). Toronto: McGraw-Hill Ryerson.

107. P. Sanger, Blind Faith, supra note

107a. Personal Communications to the author from several intervenors to the Port Granby hearings while doing research on the social impacts of the inquiry process on the Port Hope area, March 1982.

108. For a review of the early experience with public participation in NEPA, see E. Gellhorn, "Public Participation in Administrative Proceedings" in M. Blissett (ed) Environmental Impact Assessment (1976). New York: New York Engineering Foundation. Another critical review of American experience with public participation in Larry Canter, "Public Participation in Environmental Decision-Making" In: Environmental Impact Assessment (1977). Toronto: McGraw-Hill Book Co; at p. 220.

109. Hickey v. Electric Reductions Co. (1970), 21 D.L.R. (3d) 368 (NFLD. S.C.).

110. Gellhorn, "Public Participation", supra note

111. For example, during the Berger Inquiry CARC circulated a monthly newsletter, Northern Perspectives to more than ten thousand Canadians. The newsletter provided critical material for the media and often reprinted submissions made by CARC and other interest groups participating to the Inquiry in their entirety. Similarly, the CWF published a bi-weekly newsletter entitled "Pipeline Update" which dealt exclusively with the NEB hearings. It was sent to more than two hundred thousand members and served to put pressure on the Trudeau Liberals to recognize the environmental concerns of the CWF. Finally, and perhaps most importantly, both the Anglican and United Churches in Canada also published newsletters, distributed books and showed movies on the Mackenzie Valley Pipeline proposal. All this activity served to solidify the position of these interest groups and rationalize the importance of their interventions in public decision-making on major development projects.

112. See F. Anderson, NEPA and the Courts (1978). Englewood Cliffs, N.J.: Prentice-Hall Inc.

113. R. F. Keith, D. W. Fisher and others. Northern

Development and Technology Assessment Systems: A Study of Petroleum Development Programs (1976). Report prepared for the Science Council of Canada. Ottawa: Ministry of Supply and Services.

114. See discussion, infra, pp.

115. Ray Silver, "Everybody Pays Soaring Cost of Public Hearings" (1980), Financial Post, (Aug. 30) p. 13.

116. Lane Davis, "The Cost of the New Realism" in H. S. Kariel (ed) Frontiers of Democratic Theory (1970).

117. G. Rogers and J. Halpern, A Process for Siting Hydrocarbon Facilities on the Canadian Arctic Coast (1982). Ottawa: Environment Canada and Indian and Northern Affairs Canada.

118. For background, see "Shared authority of NEB, government referred to sometimes as chaotic in U. S.". The Globe and Mail, January 25, 1975, p.

119. Ibid.

120. See A. R. Lucas and T. Bell, The National Energy Board: Policy, Procedure and Practice (1977). A Study Prepared for the Law Reform Commission of Canada. Ottawa: Minister of Supply and Service; at p. 123-4.

121. J. Sokalosky, "The Canada -U.S. Alaska Highway Pipeline: A Study in Environmental Decision-Making" (1979), American Review of Canadian Studies,

122. For an example, see M. Purdue and R. Kemp, "A Case for Funding Objectors and Public Inquiries? A Comparison of the Position in Canada as opposed to the United Kingdom", [1985] Planning and Environment Law 675.

In view of this review of public *parti*cipation I would contend that Berger promoted a new mode of public involvement in decision-making in Canada during the Mackenzie Valley Pipeline Inquriy which addressed the very problem that Wicklien describes. Due to Berger's efforts and the support of the media, the Canadian Public were forced to take notice. In the process attitudes towards public policy were changed. It appeared that people, even vulnerable groups like the Inuit and Indians, could influence decisions made by *bureaucrats* and politicians. Moreover, governments took notice and were forced to increase their commitment to public involvement in government decision-making. This has subsequently proven to have been an important episode in our history as a nation because it taught politicians that the public does have something to contribute to policy-making decision-making outside of the sphere of electoral politics.

There other reasons to support intervenor funding though. Set against the context of advocacy advertising in the modern media, public interest intervention also has an important balancing effect on public perceptions about big business and their relationship to government. Following many public relations disasters related to environmental issues in the 1970s (e.g. Three Mile Island, Love Canal), advocacy advertising became an important corporate technique for explicating policies and rationalizing enormous profits. (289) Recently, corporations have begun to expand the use of this technique even more to lobby government for policies they desire and "educate the public".

123. For a particulary good exposition on the Alaskan Inquiry, See Anderson, NEPA and the Courts, supra, note 112.

123a. A general survey of U.S. experience with enforcement of environmental laws is preented in Thomas P. Gallagher, "Enforcement and Compliance Approaches of the United States Environmental Protection Agency" (1985), in L. Duncan (ed.) Environmental Enforcement: Proceedings of the National Conference on the Enforcement of Environmental Law. Edmonton: Environmental Law Centre.

124. Page, Northern Development, supra, note 2, pp. 89-123. Another useful source on the conception of the process and the plan to provide funding is W. R. D. Sewell, "How Canada Responded: The Berger Inquiry" in T. O'Riordan and W. R. D. Sewell (eds), Project Appraisal and Policy Review (1981). New York: John Wiley and Sons; at p. 93.

125. Page, ibid.

126. E. Dosman, The National Interest: The Politics of Northern Development, 1968 - 1975 (1976). Toronto: McClelland and Stewart. Hereinafter: Dosman, National Interest.

127. The Terms of Reference for the Inquiry did not specifically indicate that Berger was to provide intervenor funding. However, Berger was empowered to "bring before him any person whose attendance he considers necessary to the inquiry, examine such persons under oath, compel the production of documents and do all things necessary to provide a full and proper inquiry." Moreover, Berger was permitted to engage the servies of technical experts as required, provided with money to rent space and hire Counsel at Treasury Board rates, and designated a DIAND officer to coordinate the work of the Inquiry. Given this mandate Berger was able to make a strong case to Treasury Board for intervenor funding. For the Terms of Reference, see Privy Council Order P.C. 1974-641 dated March 21, 1974. Reprinted in Berger, Inquiry, "Appendices", supra note 2.

128. Easton's model is presented in M. Taylor, Health Insurance and Canadian Health Policy (1968). Montreal: McGill-Queen's University Press. As Taylor contends, decisions can be analysed in terms of a systems framework which identifies several types of factors that contribute to a decision (i.e. input, withinput, output, outcomes, and feedback). This system is illustrated below:

Easton's Model of Decision-Making as modified
from Taylor

Filter

Inputs ──→ Withinputs ──→ Outputs ──→ Outcomes

In the context of the Berger Inquiry the most important input would have been the original proposal from CAG. The decision by the federal government to hold the Inquiry would be a withinput. The reports produced and the awareness generated in southern Canada about the north could be seen as outputs. The decision not to go ahead with the pipeline was an outcome, and the hearing process itself was the major vehicle for feedback.

129. On September 8, 1977, Prime Minister Trudeau announced Cabinet's decision not to permit the construction of the Mackenzie Valley Pipeline. Instead the government approved the proposal to build the Alaska Highway Pipeline as recommended in the NEB Report. This latter proposal was also subject to public review: See discussion, infra, pp.

130. Canadian Arctic Gas argued that Canada faced an imminent natural gas shortage but that we could nevertheless continue to export gas to the United states. The large size of the pipeline was intended to defray the construction costs and exports would allow exports to take place and simultaneously supply the Canadian market: Page, Northern Development, supra note 2.

131. Ibid.

132. See Department of Finance, "A Northern Canadian Gas Pipeline: Evaluation of the Impact on the Economy" (1973) Canadian Forum, June/July 1973, p. 16. This version was leaked to Canadian Form. It appears that this leak was an attempt by the Department of Finance to fight breaucratic support for the project. See D. Cohen, "Ottawa Energy Studies seen as just ego trips" Toronto Star December 5, 1973. According to Cohen, the situation at the time was this: "Finance is anti-development of the North, the resources department and energy board are gung-ho for development."

133. Background on the formation of the Task Force is provided by Dosman, The National Interest, supra note 126. As Dosman contends, the Trudeau government perceived that northern sovereignity was threatened by the Prudhoe Bay discovery and the desire of Americans to use the Northwest Passage for shipping oil to the United States. Additional background on the threat to Canada's sovereignty is provided in Dosman's articles "The Northwest Passage for Shipping oil to the United States" and "The Northern Sovereignty Crisis, 1968-1970" in E. J. Dosman (ed.) The Arctic in Question (1975). Toronto: Oxford University Press.

134. Dosman, The National Interest, ibid p. 24

135. Ibid, pp. 107-108.

136. Ibid, p. 131. As a confirmation of the extent of government involvemnt in the proposal, the CDC announced its

intent to invest $100 million in Arctic Gas before the NEB had even approved its application as a Canadian energy company. This suggests the Trudeau Cabinet had made an informal commitment to development of the project to the consortium even before the pipeline planning process had begun.

137. E. Gray, "Why Canada Needs the Arctic Gas Pipeline" in P. Pearse (ed.) The Mackenzie Pipeline (1974). Toronto: McClelland and Stewart; pp. 33-34.

138. D. Peacock, People, Peregrines and Arctic Pipelines (1977). Vancouver: Douglas and McIntyre; p.11.

139. Dosman, The National Interest, supra, note 126.

140. David Lewis, Louder Voices: The Corporate Welfare Bums (1972). Toronto: James Lewis and Samuel.

141. Calder v. Attorney-General of British Columbia (1973), 34, D.L.R. (3d) 145 (S.C.C.). For an accessible account on this episode in Canadian Indian policy, see the recent book by Daniel Raunet, Without Surrender, Without Consent: A History of the Nishaga Land Claims (1984). Toronto: Douglas and McIntyre. According to Raunet, the Nishgas sought to prove that their title had never been legally dissovled. The claim was rejected on a technicality but significantly the court split three to three on the substantive issue of whether the native title had or had not been "lawfully extinguished". Following this decision the Minister of DIAND announced that the government would deal with both "specific claims" (relating to grievances based on statute or administration thereof) and "comprehensive claims" (relating to claims supported by traditional native occupancy of land). This then was a major breakthrough on Indian policy that could not have timed in a worse way for a Liberal government bent on developing the North.

142. B. Richardson, Strangers Devour the Land: The Cree Hunters of the James Bay Area versus Premier Bourassa and James Bay Development Corporation (1976). Toronto: McClelland and Stewart.

143. The Task Force on Northern Oil Development recognized the possibility that land claims might have to be dealt with but DIAND was not prepared to make any settlements: for discussion on this, see Dosman, The National Interest, supra note 126 at p. 123-4. According to Dosman, Cabinet wanted to avoid an Alaskan-type settlement. At the same time, the spectre of native claims had been brought into sharper focus by the Calder case. This forced the Trudeau Liberals to reckon with the claims being made by native groups and might have partially forced Justice Minister Turner to appoint Berger as Commissioner.

144. As a practicing lawyer, Berger had defended native people in numerous criminal matters in the early 1960s. These experiences motivated him to get involved with land claims.

Eventually he argued the well known case which eventually led him to argue the breakthrough case on aboriginal title in Canada, Calder, supra note 111, before the British Columbia Court of Appeal. Berger's reflections on the case are presented in his autobiographical essay on the case in Fragile Freedoms: Human Rights and Dissent in Canada. (1981). Toronto: Irwin.

145. The Berger Inquiry was extremely helpful to the southern media. An information officer was appointed and a press kit (containing biographical information on Berger and the Commission counsel, a copy of the Order-in-Council establishing the Inquiry and a copy of the "Expanded Guidelines" for the intervenor groups and so on) was issued. In addition, copies of the daily transcripts of the hearings were made available in Ottawa, Toronto, and Vancouver. This approach served the print media very well and allowed newspapers and magazines to publish articles with accompanying maps (some of them in colour). Thus readers of the print media were able to familiarize themselves with the issues. However, this approach did not serve the electronic media as well, primarily because the issues involved were extremely complex. While Peter Gzowski's "Morningside" could bring considerable depth to analysis of the issues and regularly did, television editors did not consider the Inquiry exciting viewing unless native groups threatened to blow up the pipeline. This might have encouraged native groups to exaggerate their claims in the same way that modern terrorists exploit the media today to build support for their causes.

146. See discussion, infra pp.

147. See F. Bregha, supra, note 2, p. 19. Bregha's point may be challenged on the ground that many other groups who spoke before Berger raised concerns about the envorinment. This touches on an issue dealth with infra at pp. CARC would also claim that it is not merely an environmental group but one concerned with the wise use of resources.

148. Ibid, p. 18.

149. See Page, Northern Development, supra note 2.

150. For further discussion, see D. McRobert "The Consequences of Balanced Development in Northern Canada: The Ecological Implications of an Exotic Ideology", Major Paper, Faculty of Environmental Studies, York University, August 1984.

151. For an excellent survey of the impact of the intervenor funding on the politics of the Inquiry and the socio-economic information presented to it, see D. Torgerson Industrialization and Assessment: Social Impact Assessment as a Social Phenomena (1980). Downsview, Ontario: President's Advisory Committee on Northern Studies, York University. The sections of this book that examine the Berger Inquiry may just be the most interesting critique of the Inquiry that has ever been written.

152. See E. L. Knowles and I. G. Waddell (eds), _The Mackenzie Valley Pipeline Inquiry: Preliminary Materials_. (1975). Ottawa: DIAND. These materials were prepared for the benefit of the general public but were regarded as too complex by many people who worked in native communities preparing for the hearings. Thus, they felt it was necessary to supplement the education of the public with very political broadcasts on the CBC Northern Service which described the pipeline project as grandiose and unrealistic. No doubt this form of "public education" influenced the perceptions of those elders that spoke eloquently at the public hearings in the communities. For further discussion, see F. Abele,

153. For a critical review of the National Energy Board's approach to the Mackenzie Pipeline decision and its refusal to fund public interest intervenors, see J. Robinson, "Policy, Pipelines and Public Participation: The National Energy Board's Northern Pipeline Decision" in O. Dwivedi (ed.), _Resources and the Environment, supra_ note .

154. F. Bregha, "The Mackenzie Valley Pipeline and Canadian Natural Gas Policy" (1977), _Canadian Public Policy_

155. National Energy Board. _Reasons for Decision: Northern Pipelines_ (1977) Ottawa: Minister of Supply and Services. For a critical discussion of the NEB decision, see F. Bregha, _Bob Blair's Pipeline_ (1979). Toronto: James Lorimer.

156. The NEB must base its conclusion on the evidence it receives. Thus, the Board might have been able to conclude the Arctic Gas proposal was acceptable if the public interest interventions had not been made. See Lucas and Bell, _The National Energy Board, supra_ note

157. NEB, _Northern Pipelines, supra_ note 155, p. 152.

157a. Dosman, _supra_ note 126, pp.

158. Page, _Northern Development, supra_, pp. 91-93.

159. Bregha, "Ten Year Muddle", _supra_ note 2, pp. 18-19.

160. J. Livingston, _Arctic Oil: The Destruction of the North?_ (1981). Toronto: CBC Publishing.

161. See R. Silver, _supra_.

162. Page, _Northern Development_, pp. 90-91

163. D. Loubser, _Development Centred on Man: Some Relevant Concepts from Canada_, (1980). Report to UNESCO and UNEP. Paris: UNESCO.

164. On this point see D. McRobert, "A Dismal Response" (1986), _Policy Options_.

165. For an introduction to the Ontario Royal Commission on the Northern Environment (ORCNE), see Mr. Justice E. P. Hartt, Interim Report and Recommendations, The Royal Commission on the Northern Environment. April 4, 1978. The Final Report for the ORCNE was issued in August 1985 after Hartt was replaced by J.J. Fahlgren in 1978. See J. J. Fahlgren, Final Report and Recommendations (1985). Toronto: Queen's Printer. Whether public participation in this case was merely a smokescreen for a government unwilling to come to grips with the difficult problems of forestry management in Northern Ontario is unclear. However, as Anand and Scott, "Financing Public Participation", supra note 7 at p. 107, observe, one person remarked that "the complexity of [the ORCNE] structure and activity has effectively overshadowed its substantive work."

166. Public participation and intervenor for the Commission were authorized under Order-in-Council 1900/77. The total funds allocated were $2.5 million. However, not all the funds were used: see discussion in D. H. Access Research Associates Inc., Beaufort Sea Environmental Assessment and Review Process Intervenor Funding Program Comparative Study: Final Report, (1985). Ottawa: Evaluation Branch, DIAND; pp.

167. Lucas and Bell, supra note

168. Ibid

169. See I. Blue, "Costs and Intervenor Funding -- The National Energy Board", in N. Bankes and J. O. Saunders, (eds.) Public Disposition of Natural Resources, (1984). Essays from the First Banff Conference on Natural Resources Law, Banff, Alberta April 12-15, 1983. Calgary: Canadian Institute of Resources Law.

170. FEARO, Revised Guide to the Federal Environmental Assessment and Review Process (1979). Ottawa: Ministry of Supply and Services.

171. "Federal Projects" are those initiated by federal departments and agencies, those for which Federal fundss have been sollicited and those involving Federal land or property. Accordingly 99% of the projects in the NWT and the YT would come under the EARP. For an outline of these lands, see FEARO, Revised Guide, ibid.

172. FEARO and EARP were creatures of an Order-in-Council passed in 1974 and then revised under the Government Organization Act in 1984.

174. Canada, House of Commons. Parliamentary Debates, 2nd Session, 29th Parliament, Vol. 1 (1974), p. 499.

174. W. J. Couch, J. F. Herity and R. E. Munn, Environmental Impact Assessment in Canada (1981). Occasional Paper No. 6, Ottawa: FEARO.

175. FEARO does not assess the screening results for EIAs. This task is handled by the Department of the Environment and other related federal deparments such as Fisheries and Oceans.

176. As a data collection method for assessment and evaluation of project options, impact statments are not new. In fact, it could be argued they have been undertaken in Canada for at least 50 years. for three precedents which support this contention, see W. J. Couch et al., Environmental Impact Assessment in Canada, supra note 174 at p. 1-2.

177. A critical discussion on this point is presented in R. Lang, "Environmental Impact Assessment: Reform or Rhetoric" in W. Leiss (ed), Ecology versus Politics in Canada (1979). Toronto: University of Toronto.

178. A. R. Lucas, D. Macleod and R. S. Miller, "Regulation of High Arctic Development: Policy Framework and Priorities" (1979). In: Marine Transportation and High Arctic Development: Policy Framework and Priorities. Symposium Proceedings, 21-23 March, 1979, Montebello, Que. Ottawa: CARC; pp. 99-209.

179. Hon. J. Fraser, Minister of the Environment. Statement made to interviewer for "Arctic Oil", A Canadian Broadcasting Corporation documentary produced in 1980 for "The Nature of Things."

180. See "Assessor comes under Procedural Scrutingy", 4(2) ECOLOG: Monthly Report on Canadian Pollution Legislation, February 1987. See also "Minister Calls Environmental Review a "woefully inadequate" process," The Globe and Mail, January 13, 1987, p. A5.

181. W.E. Rees, Reflections on the Environmental Assessment and Review Process (EARP): A Discussion Paper (1979). CARC Working Paper No. 1. Ottawa: Canadian Arctic Resources Committee.

182. D. P. Emond, Environmental Assessment Law (1978). Toronto: Emond-Montgomery.

183. D. P. Emond, "Fairness, Efficiency and FEARO: An Analysis of EARP" (1984) in E. S. Case, P. Finkle and A. R. Lucas (eds.), Fairness in Environmental and Social Impact Assessment Process. Proceedings of a Seminar convened by the Canadian Institute of Resources Law and FEARO (Vancouver Office), February 1-3, 1983. Calgary: CIRL; pp. 49-75.

184. D. Peacock, People, Peregrines and Arctic Resources, supra note ---.

185. K. Lysyk, E. Bohmer and E. Phelps. Alaska Highway Pipeline Inquiry (1977). Ottawa: Ministry of Supply and Services. For comments on the Inquiry, see Emond, Environmental Assessment Law, supra, note 182.

186. Lysyk et al., ibid, p. 141.

187. H. Faulkner, (Something like) "The Impact of Intervenors on Public Policy" (1980), Canadian Public Administration.

188. In one sense Dosman's prediction was accurate. Certainly the Cabinet did not repeat the "mistake" of giving subsequent northern inquiries the powers it had given Berger. For example, an application was made by Foothills to construct the Alaska Higway Pipeline in September 1976 but it was not until April 1977 that Terms of Reference were provided to K. Lysyk, a law professor at the University of British Columbia and E. Hill to establish inquiries on the socio-economic and environmental impacts dimensions of the proposal respectively. Moreover, the inquiries were given barely three months to complete their work whereas Berger had nearly three years. Finally, in splitting the socio-economic and environmental aspects of the application a vital dimension of EIA was deliberately finessed and controversy avoided.

189. The environmental component of the EARP had submitted its report on July 28, 1977. Although the report acknowledged that a short lead time had been available, it concluded that the Alaskan Highway route was preferable to Mackenzie Valley route. In addition, it recognized that the environmental impact of a pipeline down the Dempster Highway (not yet completed at the time was unknown. See E. Hill et al. Alaska Highway Pipeline: Environmental Concerns (1977). Ottawa: Ministry of Supply and Services.

190. See Discussion, infra pp.

191. FEARO, Environmental Assessment Panel; Arctic Pilot Project Northern Component: Report of the Environmental Assessment Panel (1980). Ottawa: Ministry of Supply and Services.

For a review to the application of the EARP in the Lancaster Sound region, see T. Nesbitt, Northern Assessment: A Play within a Play. Major Paper, Faculty of Environmental Studies, York University, April 1982.

192. Panel, Lancaster Sound, p. 80. In addition to these two recommendations, the Panel also recommended that FEARO establish an appropriate mechanism to monitor the degree to which the Panel's recommendations were implemented. However, since the Lancaster Sound drilling project was abandoned this was not necessary.

193. D. W. I. Marshall, Vice-Chairman Lancaster Sound Environmental Assessment Panel. Letter to Hon. L. Marchand, Minister of the Environment dated February 12, 1979. Reprinted in FEARO, Lancaster Sound Drilling: Report of the Environmental Assessment Panel (1979). Ottawa: Ministry of Supply and Services.

194. P. Jacobs, _Lancaster Sound Regional Study: Report on the Public Review Phase_ (1982). Ottawa: DIAND

195. Ewan Cotterill, "Major Frontier Project Approval: The Government View" (1981). FEARO Occasional Paper No. 5. Ottawa: FEARO.

195. See W. Rees, "Northern Land Use Planning -- In Search of a Policy" (1984) in _National and Regional Interests in the North_. Proceedings of the Third National Workshop on People, Resources and the Environment North of 60 degrees, Yellowknife, NWT, 1-3, June 1983. Ottawa: CARC; pp.199-234.

196. N. M. Simmons, J. Doniheee and H. Monaghan, "Planning for Land Use in the North West Territories" in R. Olson, F. Geddes and R. Hasting (eds). _Northern Ecology and Resource Management_ (1984). Edmonton: The University of Alberta.

198. J. Habermas, _Legitimation Crisis_ (1975). Boston: Beacon.

199. For discussion on proactive planning as a technique for public participation, see D. P. Emond, "Comment" in N. Bankes and J. O. Saunders (eds), _Public Disposition of Natural Resources_ (1984). Essays from the First Banff Conference on Natural Resources Law, Banff, Alberta April 12-15, 1983. Calgary: Canadian Institute of Resources Law.

200. Cotterill, "Major Frontier Project Approval", _supra_ note 195.

201. Consultation for the Beaufort EARP was undertaken as soon as the project was referred by Dome Petroleum to the lead Agency, DIAND. This consultation was intended to arouse interest and to identify issues and concerns. Accordingly, all native groups with an interest in the north, most communities in the Mackenzie Delta, in the Valley and on Baffin Island, all major environmental non-governmental organizations, all federal departments and the territorial governments were contacted by FEARO.

202. The panel members also held workshops in all the affected remote communities to help imporve the intervention and research skills of the local population. This paid off later because it enhanced the quality of submissions made by a number of these communities at the hearings held in the fall of 1984.

203. FEARO, _Interim Report: Beaufort Sea Hydrocarbon Prodution and Transport_ (1982). Vancouver: FEARO.

204. _First and Second Compendia of Written Submisions to the Environmental Assessment Parel on the Dome, Gulf and Esso Environmental Impact Statement_ (1983). Vancouver: FEARO.

205. FEARO _Beaufort Sea Hydrocarbon Production and Transportation: Final Report of the Environmental Assessment_

Panel (1984). Ottawa: Ministry of Supply and Services.

206. For a critical review of the whole Beaufort EARP, see "Not with a Bang, but a BEARP", Northern Perspectives December 1984.

207. Nordicity Group and Boreal Ecology Ltd., Beaufort Sea EARP Intervenor Funding Program Evaluation: Final Report (1985). Ottawa: Program Evaluation Branch, DIAND. Hereinafter: Nordicity Group, Evaluation.

208. The Assistant Deputy Minister of the Northern Affairs division of DIAND remained legally responsible for the funds although FEARO administered them: Nordicity Group, ibid.

209. FEARO, Beaufort Final Report, supra note 205.

210. Ibid.

210. Ibid.

211. The public interest group coalition broke up most of the money they were allocated int small research contracts. Some of the people who participated ir. the evaluation of the funding programme felt that the value of this research was dubious in some cases: see Nordicity Grcup, Evaluation, supra note 207.

212. As reported in "A question of priniciple: Beaufort Sea Research Coalition disbands," Northern Perspectives, 10(4): 12. The Coalition, which was made of five environmental groups, was informed after receiving support for six months that funding would be slashed by 62 percent to $100,000 per year. In the view of some of the groups that had originally agreed to participate, this was totally inadequate. Accordingly, CARC dropped out and provided the following rationale:

> We found ourselves facing a serious dilemma. To "soldier on" with reduced funding on the theory that anything is better than nothing would give legitimacy to subsequent government and corporate assertions that the public interest had been fully and fairly represented. Yet to pull out completely would leave us open to charges we were acting irresponsibly.

> The reduced sum of $100,000, though substantial, was inadequate against the task at hand. As well, it would have been impossible to plan research and programmes over an extended period when funding levels were so erratic. No industry or government agency could work effectively with roller-coaster funding. Neither could we.

With CARC gone, another group was formed called the Beafort Sea Alliance. It attempted to carry the mantle of the original coalition but it was only partly successful as suggested already in note 211.

213. Nordicity Group, Evaluation, supra, note 207.

214. FEARO, "Funding of Public Participation in the Environmental Assessment Review of Military Flying Activities in Labrador and Quebec," Press Release, January 30, 1987., Ottawa, Ont. For background on the issues involved, see P. Armitage, "Environment and Innu Culture Versus Nato" (1986), 9(1) Probe Post 14.

215. Apart from the problems that adminstrators sometimes voice about the methodological barriers to public participation, often a deeper psychological matter is at issue. In essence, planners and administrators fear they will lose power and prestige when the public is involved in decision-making to a greater degree. This does not appear to be a valid reason to decrease the importance of public involvement, however.

216. H. Kunreathers and J. Lathrop, "Siting Hazardous Facilities: Lessons from LNG" (1981), 1(4) Risk Analysis 289.

217. A leading American text on the methodological problems related to public participation and facility siting is E.A. Williams and A.K. Massa, Siting of Major Facilities: A Practical Approach (1983). New York: McGraw-Hill.

218. Kasperson, supra note 44 has identified four major components in environmental decision-making: 1) knowledge and awareness of the disputed resource; 2) attitudes towards political system; 3) role of collective action; and 4) policy formulation and political participation (especially by special interest groups). Kasperson contends, at p. 177, that the first two underpin the latter two. The issue that arises is how do knowledge and awareness of the resource and attitudes towards politics influence participation. Kasperson shows that these can act as potential barriers to the reformation of policies on public participation, which are determined in relation to the latter two factors.

219. See M. O'Hare, L. Bacon and D. Sanderson, Facility Siting and Public Opposition (1983). New York: Van Nostrand Reinhold.

220. N. Wengert, "Where can we go with Public Participation in the Planning Process?" in Dworsky, Alleee and Csallary (eds.) National Symposium supra note 45, p. 10.

221. The resistance has been driven by the Canadian Environmental Law Association (CELA). For background, see article on Donald Chant in Harrowsmith.

K. A. Concannon, "A Public Involvment Strategy for Siting Transmission Lines: Two Case Studies" in Facility Siting and Routing, 1984 Energy and Environment (1984). Proceedings of an International Conference at Banff, Alberta. Banff: Banff Centre School of Management.

223. A. Armour, "Issue Managment in Resource Planning" in R. Lang (ed) Integrated Approaches to Resource Planning (1986). Calgary: University of Calgary Press.

224. This arguments rests on the fact that heavy capital investments are usually made and this may present a large opportunity cost: see Ray Silver, supra note

225. Under s. 7 of the EAA, any person may inspect an environmental assessment of an undertaking and make a written submission to the Minister with respect to the undertaking and the EA. In the submission, a hearing may be requested but the Minister is granted full discretion to determine whether hearing is required. Thus, under s. 12 (2) (b) the Minister can refuse further public involvement when he considers the public requirement to be "frivolous or vexatious or that a hearing is unnecessary or may cause undue delay."

226. Under Ontario's EAA, public involvment is initiated through Ministerial notice under s. 7(1) (b). No specific notice must jbe given to adjacent landowners under the Act; this requirement is found under s. 39(12) and 39(17) of the Planning Act R.S.O. 1980 C. 379. In major projects where both these statutes are likely to be invoked, the governing legislation is the Consolidated Hearings Act S.O. 1981, C. 20, S. 7.

227. See R. E. Munn (ed), Environmental Impact Assessment. SCOPE 5, 2nd ed. (1979). Toronto: John Wiley and Sons.

228. Lang and Armour, "Process". See also the chapter on Public Participation in R. Lang and A. Armour (eds) Environmental Planning Resourcebook (1980). Montreal: Multiscience.

229. For discussion of this point in the context of multi-disciplinary planning, see J. R. Galbraith and D. A. Nathanson Strategy Implementation: The Role of Structure and Process (1978). Boulder, Colorado: West Publishing Company.

229a. Page, supra note 2, pp.

230. For background on the NIMBY Syndrome, see the volume edited by A. Armour, (ed), The Not-In-My-Backyard Syndrome. Proceeding from a Two-day Symposiujm on Public Involvment in Siting WAste Management Facilities, 13-14 May 1983 (1984). Downsview: Faculty of Environmental Studies, York University. For an accessible summary of the key arguments, see E. Farkas, "The NIMBY Syndrome" (1982), 10(2/3) Alternatives. It should be noted that one must be careful in criticzing those who succumb to the NIMBY Syndrome. After all, they are usually responding to a percived threat to their economic worth posed by a reduction in the value of their homes. Philosophically this postion is deeply entrenched in the Lockean paradigm of property. See R. W. G. Bryant, Land: Private Property, Public Control (1972). Montreal: Harvest House.

230a. McRobert, _supra_ note

231. see K. C. Bowen and J. I. Harris, "Problems with People, Decision, Conflict, Language and Measurement" in D. F. Burkhardt and W. H. Ittelson (eds) _Environmental Assessment of Socio-economic Systems_ (1978). New York: Plenum Press

232. McRobert, "Canada and the World Conservation Strategy", _supra_, note _ p. .

233. Rachelle Alterman, "Planning for Public Particiption: The Design of Implementable Strategies" (1982), 9 _Environment and Planning B_ 295.

234. Wengert's view are presented in his article "Public Participation in Water Planning: A Critique of Theory, Doctrine and Practice" (****), 7(1) _Water Resources Bulletin_ 26. For an interesting response, see J. Pierce and Harvey R. Doerksen. _Water Politics and Public Involvement_ (1976). Ann Arbor, Michigan: Ann Arbour Science Publications.

235. Wengert, "Where do we go with Public Participation", _supra_ note __ .

236. _Ibid_.

237. Wengert, "Public Participation," _supra_, note 234, p. 26.

238. For a critique of public hearings as a vehicle for public participation, see B. Checkoway, "Public Hearings are not Enough" (1980) in _Citizen Participation_, May/June 1980.

239. J. Habermas, _Towards a Rational Society_ (1971). Trans. Jeremy J. Shapiro. Boston: Beacon Press. See also, Torgerson, _Industrialization and Assessment, supra_ note 151.

240. G. Szablowski, _Public Bureaucracy and the Possibility of Citizen Involvement in the Government of Ontario_ (1971).

241. _Ibid_ at p.

242. In this context "marginalization" refers to a process whereby a grop of people lose control over development and become mere observers of their own social and cultural collapse. In this case it was argued that the lack of a land claims settlement exacerbated the marginalization of the Inuit in so far as it prevented access to capital and didn't encourage preparation of an alternative scenario for development in the region. For discussion, see H. Brody, _The Peoples Land_ (1975). Markham: Penguin.

243. M. Edelman, _The Symbolic Uses of Politics_ (1964). Urbana: University of Illinois Press.

244. On equivalence problems, see E. Laclau and C. Mouffe,

Hegemony and Socialist Strategy: Towards a Radical Democratic Politics (1985). Translated by Winston Moore and Paul Cammack. London: Verso.

245. See discussion, infra pp.

246. See discussion procedures in Quebec and Ontario in E. S. Case et al, (eds.), Fairness, supra note 183.

246a. The leading Canadian scholar on constitutional dimensions of environmental jurisdictional is Dale Gibson. Two of his papers are: "The Environment and the Constitution: New Wine Old Bottles" in O. F. Dwiveci (ed) Protecting the Environment (1974). Toronto: Copp-Clark; and

247. Confusion or duplication in EIA activities in various jurisdictions has been avoided through stressing communication between the federal and provincial governments. In addition, the Canadian Council of Resource and Environment Ministers was established in 1971. This body consisted of the Minister responsible for environmental matters from the federal and each provincial jurisdiction. Under the rubric of the CCREM, senior environmental assessment administrators meet regularly to discuss issues and exchange ideas. In addition, the group has also sponsored a comprehensive survey of themain characteristics of the different Canadian EIA processes. This information is collected in W. J. Couch (ed), Environmental Assessment in Canada (1983). Ottawa: FEARO. For background on the CCREM, see Task Force on Environmental Impact Assessment, Canadian Council of Resource and Environment Ministers. Canadian Environmental Impact Assessment Process: A Discussion Paper. (1978). Ottawa: CCREM.

248. Deregulation was one of President Carter's campaign promises in 1976. He contended that deregulation was the way to eliminate the enormous burden of government paperwork paid for by the American citizenry. Soon after he was elected Carter appointed a Commission on Government Paper work. This study estimated the redtape and paperwork costed industry more than $100 million annually. In addition, it was argued that government regulation had produced monopolies in tranportation and other sectors of the economy and this had spurred inflation.

The first area where deregulation was applied in the United States was the transportation industry. It was argued that unfetterd competition forced companies to lower their freight rates, providing huge savings for shippers and consumers. Accordingly, deregulation was introduced in the railroad industry (throgh the Railroad Revitalization Regulation Reform Program) and the Airline industry (through the Airline Deregulation Act). These changes proved very popular and began to effect the changes sought. As a result, Congress passed into a law a third major reform, the Motor Carrier Act. In the aggregate these reforms have lowered costs for consumers considerably. Nevertheless, concerns about safety have been raised after numerous airplane crashes in the United States and it is unclear what the result of this deregulation process will prove to be in the long term. For further discussion, see Economic Council of Canada, Reforming Regulation (1981). Ottawa: Ministry of Supply and Services. Background on American developments is provided in G. C. Eads and M. Fix, Relief or Reform? Reagan's Regulatory Dilemma (1984). Washington: The Urban Institute Press.

249. For discussion, see McRobert "Canada and the World Conservation Strategy" supra note pp. . For a description of recent attempts on the part of Environment Canada to respond to demands for decentralization and meet local needs, see M. P. Brown "Environment Canada and the Pursuit of Administrative Decentralization" (1986), 29(2) Canadian Public Administration 218.

250. Macdonald Commission.

251. P. N. Nemetz, W. T. Stanbury and F. Thompson, "Social Regulation in Canada: An overview and Comparison with American Model" (1986), 14(4) Policy Studies Journal 580

252. For discussion on this point, see K. A. Kemp, "Lawyers, Politics and Economic Regulation" (1986), 67(3) Social Science Quarterly 267.

253. See Page, Northern Development, supra note 2 pp.

254. On this point, see J. Swaigen, How to fight for What's Right: A Citizen's Guide to Public Interest Law (1981).

255. Many of these problems stemmed from the transfer of experience in the courts to public hearings. In particular, rules of administrative law and evidence seemed to irritate groups and scientists. See ibid.

256. Ibid.

257. From the point of view of some lawyers, the EIA process is inadequate: see discussion, infra at pp. . These lawyers have argued for tightening up procedures but their views appear to have fallen largely on deaf ears until recently.

258. See "Inquiry Process", in Berger, Inquiry, Vol. 2, supra note 2. See also Page, Northern Development, supra note 2, pp. 90-91.

259. D. Fox, Public Participation in the Administrative Process (1979). A Study Prepared for the Law Reform Commission of Canada. Ottawa: LRCC.

260. Kenneth G. Englehart and M. J. Trebilcock, "Public Participation in the Regulatory Process: The Issue of Funding," (1981). Regulation Reference Working paper No 17. Ottawa: Economic Council of Canada. This is a comprehensive analysis of

different funding mechanisms.

261. Ibid.

262. Mackenzie Valley Pipeline Inquiry Statement, (August 14, 1974). Cited in A. Lucas and B. McCallum, "Looking at Environmental Impact Assessment" in P. S. Elder (ed) Environmental Management and Public Participation (1975). For addition background on the allocation process, see "Commissioner Berger Establishes Critera for Funding Intervenors at the Mackenzie Valley Pipeline Inquiry" (1975), 4 C.E.L.N. 9.

263. This general eligibility criteria was asopted by many subsequent intervenor funding programs. However, one interesting variation was the criteria employed by the ORCNE. Under their eligibility criteria, applicants that involved all parties with differing views on a particular topic were encouraged to apply for funds. It is noteworthy that few groups in this category applied: See Nordicity Group, Evaluation, supra, note 207.

264. Environmental Assessment Act., S.S. 1979-1980 C. E. 10.1., S. 6. It is noteworthy that an NDP government was in power at the time and it was led by a committed socialist, Allan Blakeney.

265. Under s. 18(9) of the EAA, the EAB has the power to provide groups with expert assistants. this power has been used to support some requests for infomation but is not very useful few public hearings held. For further details see Emond, Environmental Assessment Law, supra note 182.

265a. B. Gibson, D. McDonald and B. Savan, "The Environmental Assessment Act: A Good Tool Getting Rusty, from Lack of Use" (1986), 11(6) Intervenor: The Newsletter of the Canadian Environmental Law Association 1.

266. This works both ways. Sometimes individuals in certain agencies or departments are "at war" with representative of other govenrment agencies and are only too willing to critically assess their colleagues or studies these agencies have prepared.

267. See F. Abele,

268. Goodman, supra note 174, p. 211.

269. Ibid.

270. M. Trebilcock and K. Englehart, "A Tax Credit for Public Interest Groups" (1981), Canadian Taxation (Spring 1981) 29.

271. Ibid.

272. Fox, Public Participation, supra note 259.

273. CAC, supra note 169.

274. Blue, "Intervenor Costs", supra note 169. Blue does a thorough inventory of most of the key bodies that have powers to awards costs in the environmental and resource development sphere but his key focus is on the NEB.

275. Bell Canada, supra note 8.

276. Hamilton Wentworth (Regional Mun. of) v. Hamilton-Wentworth Save the Valley Ctee Inc. (1985), 51 O. R. (2d) 23 (Div. Ct.); and Re Ontario Energy Board Act (1985), 51 O.R. (2d), 333 (Div. Ct.), Leave to Appeal to the Ontario Court of Appeal refused at 15 Admin L. R. 86 at 122.

277. L. Fox, "Annotation" to Bell Canada, supra note 208. 17 Admin. L. R. 207, p. 209.

278. D. Fox, Participation, supra note 259.

279. This matter has a bearing on the question of when to fund public participation, an issue considered in greater deatail infra, pp. .

280. See Thomsen, supra note 55 pp.

281. Habermas, Towards a Rational Society, (1971). Trans. J. Shapiro. Boston: Beacon; pp .

282. R. Lang and A. Armour. The Assessment and Review of Social Impacts (1981). Report prepared for FEARO by Lang, Armour Associates. Ottawa: Ministry of Supply Services. This pape argues for integrating Social and environmental assessment into the EARP. As the experience from the Berger Inquiry showed the physical and biological impacts of major development projects must be considered in tandem with social, economic and cultual effects. To do otherwise would render the evaluation little more than a convetional engineering assessment. For this reason it was determined that the new federal environmental assessment process must have a broad potential mandate; hence this explains the importance attached to public participation in the EARP.

283. For discussion on this, see A. Bender and D. Clink, "Public Involvement in the EIS Process" (1978), 2 Environmental Management 2.

284. The Environmental Contaminants Act S. C. (1975), c. _ was not passed until 1975. In part this legislation was a response to perceived inadequacies with existing provisions as highlighted by intervenor groups in the Berger Inquiry.

285. J. K. Galbraith, The New Industrial State (1972; 3rd edition). New York: Mentor.

286. For background on Marshall Crowe and the incidents leading up to the trial, see R. Page, Northern Development, supra note 2, pp.

287. John Wicklein, _Electronic Nightmare: The New Communications and Freedom_ (1981). New York: The Viking Press, p. 253.

288. _Ibid_.

289. See "Imperial Oil Ads Seek to Explain Profits", (1980) _Marketing Magazine_, Nov. 3, 1980.

290. Tom Messer, "Arctic Resources Group Calls for Probe into Energy Ads" (1980), _Marketing Magazine_, Sept. 15, 1980.

291. For a compendia of briefs presented by critical public interest groups on see D. Drache and D. Cameron, _The Other McDonald Report_ (1985). Toronto: James Lorimer.

292. H. McCullum and J. McCullum, _This Land is Not for Sale_ (1975).

293. Lynn McDonald, _The Party that Changed Canada: The New Democratic Party, Then and Now_ (1987). Toronto: Macmillan.

Forthcoming, _Alternatives_. *(April 1987)*

Hard _Choices_: _A_ _Life_ _of_ _Tom_ _Berger_. By Carolyn Swayze (1987).
Vancouver: Douglas and McIntyre. 237 pp., $24.95 (HC).

Reviewed by David McRobert

During the mid-1970s Tom Berger attained folk hero status in
Canadian media, academic and political circles when he headed a
federal commission established to examine the possible effects of
construction of a pipeline through the Mackenzie Valley on the
northern environment and native peoples. The fruits of that
commission included a best-selling volume titled _Northern_
Frontier, _Northern_ _Homeland_ and a recommendation that the
proposed pipeline be delayed for at least ten years. In the
process, Berger changed the course of northern history in Canada.
Moreover, his subsequent work, including a stimulating survey on
civil liberties in Canada, _Fragile_ _Freedoms_, suggests that Berger
probably will inherit F.R Scott's mantle as Canada's leading
human rights advocate.

This new biography is an attempt to chronicle the life of
Berger and provide background on the breakthroughs that he has
achieved in numerous areas of law and public policy. Swayze, a
former law student, met Berger when she was studying at the
University of Victoria. While her sense of awe for her former
teacher is apparent in _Hard_ _Choices_, Swayze seems unable to
transcend journalistic commentary in most places. In part, this
is a reflection of Berger's own reluctance to divulge many of the
personal details about his life and work that might have allowed
Swayze to capture the essence of her subject more effectively.

Despite these weaknesses, there is much in this book that
will interest those who are intrigued by Berger's dedication to
justice and minority rights and his unique work on on aboriginal
rights and environmental issues. Chapters are organized into
neat parcels that introduce the reader to Berger's diverse career
experiences as a lawyer, politician, royal commissioner,
aboriginal rights advocate and writer. At times this approach is
not entirely successful and the continuity of Berger's story is
sacrificed to Swayze's imposed structure. To this extent the
book reflects the inexperience of the author rather than the
material at hand.

As a young lawyer Berger pioneered what has now become known
as "poverty law" in law school curricula. He defended Indians
facing charges for hunting out of season and criminals who faced
imprisonment for relatively minor offences such as theft because
they had accumulated a string of minor convictions. He
challenged the _Workmen's_ _Compensation_ _Act_ in British Columbia and
his struggles led to significant changes in a harsh legislation
that failed to acknowledge the problem of industrial disease.

Recognizing that more substantial reforms were probably necessary to address many of these problems, Berger became involved in politics in the early 1960s. He was elected MP for a short stint and eventually became an MLA and leader of the B.C. New Democratic Party. After Berger was defeated in 1969 by W.A.C. Bennett (who accused him of being a proponent of Marxian socialism), he resigned his leadership.

In 1971, Berger was offered a position on the B.C. Supreme Court and, despite his youth, decided to accept. It has been suggested this was a ploy intended to keep Berger out of the hair of the Trudeau Liberals. Whatever the case, Berger proved to be a progressive jurist worthy of his appointment; many of his rulings are still studied in Canadian law schools and, according to Swayze, demonstrated Berger's facility for "abstract cerebral puzzles."

As a judge, Berger became eligible to head up royal commissions on aspects of public policy. His first appointment was Chair of a commission established by the B.C. government to examine family law. His work led to the creation of a Unified Family Court in the South Fraser Judicial District and allowed Berger to reflect his concern about the impact of child adoption practices on native families.

Berger is best known for his work on the MacKenzie Valley Pipeline Inquiry. As a process, the Inquiry served as a crucial precedent in the debate on development in Canada's North and broke important ground in the area of intervenor funding. In addition, Berger provided native peoples and environmental organizations with a forum for voicing their concerns about the massive proposal, and in doing so, presented facts to the Canadian public that persuaded many people the pipeline should not be built. By the time Northern Frontier, Northern Homeland was released in 1977, Berger was regarded by some southern journalists as the "therapist of the north." While Swayze does a competent job in describing this background to the Inquiry, her analysis seems limp and might have benefited from a more careful study of the actual commission documents and the subsequent impact of the Inquiry on other spheres of Canadian public policy.

The most interesting part of the book deals with Berger's challenge to Trudeau over the exclusion of native rights from the initial draft of the Charter of Rights and Freedoms in 1981. Berger's actions and criticisms served to invoke Trudeau's wrath, and as a former civil libertarian, Trudeau suggested that the Judicial Council should discipline a judge who appeared eager to get involved in politics.

Over the next few months, a fascinating drama unfolded. While the Judicial Council did not ask for Berger's removal, it deemed he had been "indiscrete." Berger refused to back down, arguing that a judge should not be prevented from speaking out on a matter of minority rights. However, the pressure continued from Bora Laskin, a friend of Trudeau, and ultimately Berger decided to resign from the B.C. Supreme Court.

Since his resignation Berger has resumed his work as a lawyer and a scholar and he continues to have an important impact on aboriginal rights issues in North America. In 1983 he conducted a commission investigating the Alaskan Native Claims Settlement Act. The report from that commission, titled Village Journey, created a considerable stir in Washington when it was released in 1985. In Canada, Berger has recently grabbed headlines through his advocacy on everything from hunting and trapping rights to land claims.

In the end, I could not help but feel one thing: Berger deserved better. While Swayze makes a good attempt to chronicle Berger's life, much of the richness of his past struggles seems lost. Perhaps the best we can hope for is that Berger himself will fill in the gaps left by Swayze with an autobiographical effort at some time in the near future.

David McRobert is an LLM candidate at Osgoode Hall Law School and a Fellow in the Faculty of Environmental Studies at York University in Toronto, Ontario.

attempt to emphasize both aspects in this presentation. However, things get done at the local level. It is an accumulation of local decisions and actions, for good or ill, that results in acid precipitation, CO_2 build up, or the generally high standard of pollution control across Canada.

The key to local actions is to establish that what is being done locally is not just to help someone far away, though that is a charitable thing to do, but that by doing so, you help yourself.

For example, it may seem to the coal-fired electrical generators in the Ohio Valley that they are being pressured to reduce their sulphur emissions to benefit some people in Eastern Canada who are really only interested in replacing U.S coal-fired electricity with exported Canadian hydro. However, it is difficult to believe that the immediate neighbours to thermal plants really welcome the current levels of emissions, or that neighbouring states will be willing to put up with their continuation.

The local coal mines, under existing conditions, can look to a future of contracting markets, increasingly restricted to facilities which have no concern for the level of their emissions. For the coal mining industry of the Ohio Valley to become dynamic and expansive, they need a cure for the problem of acid precipitation just as strongly as do Ontario, Quebec and the Maritimes, so that markets for their high-sulphur coal can be widened.

The key to the adoption of actions that will benefit others is the search for a local advantage to their adoption. This may sometimes have to be an advantage imposed from without, such as the avoidance of countervailing duties by the adoption of minimum ambient air and water quality standards, but the local advantage will always have to exist. The number of times it does exist will, I believe, be a pleasant surprise, but it must be actively sought out and then built upon. ▭

Alistair D. Crerar is Chief Executive Officer of the Environment Council of Alberta. Educated at the University of British Columbia, he has worked at the federal, provincial and municipal levels in the fields of regional planning, economic development, resource management and environment conservation.

By David McRobert

A Dismal Response

We must respond more adequately to the global challenge of the World Conservation Strategy we helped to launch and then neglected

One of the first actions taken by the former federal Minister of the Environment, John Roberts, after he was appointed to the position by Trudeau in the Fall of 1981, was to endorse a little-known document called the World Conservation Strategy. Roberts went on to become one of the most popular ministers in the post-Clarke era of the Trudeau Liberals. But regrettably the WCS, which has gained support from over forty countries and many United Nations agencies since it was released in 1980, remains relatively unknown in Canada.

The reasons behind this weak support for the WCS are complex. Part of the problem is the division of powers in the Canadian constitution. No clear authority over environmental issues is granted to either the federal or provincial levels of government. Consequently, all that Roberts and his successors have been willing to do is to endorse the WCS, rather than foist it on unwilling provincial counterparts.

Another problem is that the mood of policy makers shifted when the Mulroney government was swept into power with the largest majority in Canadian history in September 1984. One of these shifts in mood was in the area of industrial regulation. Environmentalists have perceived the new attitude of the Conservatives as anti-regulatory.

Both Tory ministers responsible for the Department of the Environment under the Mulroney government have adopted primarily rhetorical positions on issues such as toxins and acid rain. Thus it is not surprising that a document such as the WCS has been overlooked.

This situation should be something of an embarrassment to the Canadian media and politicians. Many prominent Canadians, such as Maurice Strong and Dr. David Munro, were closely involved in the preparation of the WCS.

Strong was Director of one of the main agencies responsible for the production of the WCS, the United Nations Environment Programme (UNEP), at the time the document was first commissioned in 1976.

Munro, now a resident of British Columbia, was Executive Director of the other principal agency responsible for production of the Strategy, the International Union for Conservation of Nature and Natural Resources. His efforts were essential in the coordination of the submissions of over 500 non-governmental organizations and more than 800 scientists who eventually contributed to the WCS.

As a result the whole document had a distinctly Canadian flavour. For example, the model of public participation recommended in the WCS was influenced by a unique Canadian experiment, the Mackenzie Valley Pipeline Inquiry, which former British Columbia Supreme Court Judge Thomas Berger headed up in the mid-seventies. No doubt the experience of individuals such as Munro and Strong played a part in the decision to use this experiment as a basis for this WCS recommendation.

The Strategy itself outlines an agenda for protecting everything from the global commons to genetic material. In part, it was conceived to find a common ground between developed and under-developed nations for measures such as the Convention on International Trade in Endangered Species of Wild Fauna and Flora (CITES). This treaty, which is 13 years old, now has over 70 member nations as signatories. CITES imposes restrictions on international trade to limit harvesting of endangered species for furs, ivory and pharmaceuticals.

The WCS also promotes the idea of sustainable use as a basis for renewable resource use. This idea is directed at balancing economic development and conservation initiatives to ensure that the rivers and lakes our children inherit from us are more than chemical cocktails.

In the light of the drama of recent months, as possible jail sentences for the executives of industrial offenders have grabbed the headlines in Ontario and the full. implications of Chernobyl are becoming apparent, such a holistic approach to resolving environmental problems seems urgently required.

In view of the apparent need for such an approach, it is reassuring that scientists such as Munro have been busy promoting the adoption of the WCS by governments in Canada and all over the world. With the release of two reports prepared by provincial conservation organizations in response to the WCS, it seems that his efforts are paying off.

The first of these reports, entitled *Prospectus for An Alberta Conservation Strategy*, was produced by the Public Advisory Committees of the Environment Council of Alberta. The second, *Towards a Conservation Strategy for Ontario*, was prepared by the Conservation Council of Ontario and attracted considerable media attention upon its release.

These two reports are a positive step towards recognition of Canada's special role, as a vast and relatively unpopulated land, in the long-term conservation of nature. Moreover, four other provinces have undertaken similar reviews of their programs to determine how much further they must go to comply with the objectives of the WCS.

Much work remains to be done to alleviate environmental problems in Canada. Both the Alberta and Ontario governments, for example, have a long way to go before their practices begin to broach the goal of sustainability as set out by the WCS.

The Ontario response to the WCS is divided into six "issue areas": agriculture; forestry; water resource management; wildlife and natural areas; waste management; and land use conflicts. Discussion of each area is divided into four subsections which outline the desired position of the Conservation Council and their priority concerns regarding future government action.

The actual work was done by six Task Forces made up of Council members. The majority of Task Force participants were conservationists with experience in either government or NGOs. But the President of the Council, Simon Miles, is quick to point out that numerous other members, representing professions such as medicine and education and groups such as labour, were also involved in the production of the final report.

In contrast, the Alberta study was produced under the rubric of three of the public advisory committees of the Environment Council of Alberta. The Council represents 130 different provincial organizations, ranging from wilderness groups to the YMCA. Their report identifies six objectives for an Alberta strategy.

These objectives include modifications of those outlined above as well as three additional ones. These relate to the provision of recreational opportunities, the maintenance of high quality of life in urban environments, and the management of non-renewable resources.

One of the most important problems facing wildlife managers in North America is the protection of wildlife habitat. Not surprisingly, this problem receives detailed consideration in both the Alberta and Ontario studies.

In the Alberta report, ensuring sustainable use is shown to be complicated by losses of wetlands, woodlots and shelterbelts to cultivation. However the *Prospectus* suggests that another parallel initiative, the Alberta Wildlife Plan, may provide the needed solutions.

The Ontario document considers the problem of wetlands preservation in terms of existing land-use policies. The Council observes that land-use decisions are being made continuously, usually in the absence of any meaningful input from wildlife managers. A major victory will have been won, they claim, if such decisions are tempered by environmental considerations in the future.

Both documents recognize, however, that the preservation of wildlife habitat is not an end-point. The demands of users, the attitudes towards poaching and the actual genetic resilience of population all have to be evaluated and taken into account by managers.

Most of this information is not very newsworthy. We know that modification and destruction of habitat is the prime cause of the decline of wildlife populations. Despite this, it is apparent that the cure is not as easily identified and implemented as the illness is diagnosed. And the slow progress on habitat is only one example of this recurring theme in the Ontario and Alberta reports.

One issue which the Ontario report examines in considerable detail is sustainable utilization of Canada's forests. In terms of the framework set out in the WCS, the current governmental response to the forestry problem is to conserve those processes and portions of the natural environment that enable natural self-regulation. However, the report observes that "a false perception of plenty" has encouraged a rate of exploitation that clearly is not sustainable in the long-term.

Another area where the Ontario report is extremely critical of government policy is agricultural land conservation. The authors note that more than one million acres of Ontario's best agricultural land was lost between 1971 and 1981. They advocate that this prime land—much of it around cities and towns—be preserved rather than paved.

Alberta's *Prospectus* also calls for major changes in agricultural land use and policies, noting that the number of acres affected by erosion, dryland salinity, loss of organic matter, and soil acidification is unknown but presumed to be significant. Moreover, the report goes on to observe that "agriculture would seem to be the most obvious of all sustainable developments" and that a crucial requirement of a provincial conservation strategy is improvement and maintenance of Alberta's agricultural land base.

There are other parallels between the two documents. Both clearly emphasize the urgent need to deal with problems such as toxic pollution, acid rain and hazardous waste management. Both recognize the need not only for sound scientific data upon which to base procedures, but for strong political commitment to ensure that the good intentions already expressed will be translated into action. To this end, the reports offer a series of recommendations for action and the establishment of permanent mechanisms for monitoring this action.

The documents are also similar in emphasizing that wildlife belongs to everyone and must be uniformly accessible to all Canadians, so long as the survival of a species is not threatened. At the same time, both reports acknowledge that many species of flora and fauna are not receiving adequate protection from poachers and other forces such as development pressure. The Ontario study, for example, notes that "there is far from adequate attention to the protection of those species that are rare, threatened or endangered."

The two reports do differ in some respects. An interesting difference between the two documents is the five-page discussion of the importance of conservation of non-renewable resources in the *Prospectus*. The tone of this discussion suggests that conservation of oil, gas, oil sands, and heavy oil resources is essential to balance development in the province of Alberta. The Ontario report does not, in direct contrast, consider economic conservation arguments for mineral resources.

The ultimate impact of these remarkable volunteer efforts will depend largely on whether the public demands that Canada meet the objectives set out in the WCS. To date, the government response has been dismal. We should expect to be chastised by leaders from the Third World as hypocritical if we continue to balk at implementing the Strategy. Canada has failed to meet the challenge of global conservation, after helping to promulgate the WCS in the 1970s. There is a touch of irony in this situation. However, it is one that we should view with embarrassment rather than smugness.

David McRobert is a student at Osgoode Hall Law School and a Fellow in the Faculty of Environmental Studies at York University.

By Randal Marlin

Censoring Pornography

Law on pornography must protect the weak from exploitation and the public from offence, yet allow for local norms of tolerance and free speech

With the introduction of Bill C-114 in 1986 the government responded to the growing demands for a crackdown on pornography. These demands have come from groups normally at odds—militant feminists and tradition-oriented conservative forces. It is an unstable coalition, with widely differing philosophies, but it has produced a large measure of agreement on the elimination of hard-core pornography.

Ammunition in the form of the 1984 Badgley Report on Sexual Offences Against Children, the 1985 Fraser Committee on Pornography and Prostitution, and most recently the Attorney General's Commission on Pornography in the United States, will probably result in passage of large chunks of the bill.

Historically, Conservative governments in Canada have not been pre-eminently defensive about free speech (some of Diefenbaker's public utterances notwithstanding) and there is a good chance that knee-jerk libertarianism, abetted by the mass media who feel their own interests threatened, will not carry the day. We are, or should be, in for some of the most serious debate on

A *longer paper* on this subject by the author may be obtained at cost from the Canadian Coalition Against Media Pornography, Box 1075, Station B, Ottawa. K1P 5R1.

the question of pornography that we have yet seen in Canada. It should soon become apparent that this is now an issue on which action will be taken. What is said is likely to matter.

All the more reason, then, to review the complexity of the issues surrounding what is called, for short, the "pornography" question. As with any legislation, it is helpful to begin with Bentham's suggestions for clear thinking on the subject.

We should get clear in our minds what are the evils that the legislation is designed to remove. We then have to ask whether the particular legislation is the most effective way of dealing with the problem. Is the criminal law the best mechanism? We also have to consider what possible side-effects of an undesirable kind the particular legislation may bring with it. Will we be opening the door to suppression of other forms of expression besides the pornographic? If the basis for attaching penal sanctions to the dissemination of pornography is the ultimate harm produced by pornography, what about the perceived harms wrought by politically dissentient speech? Where do you draw the line?

These are not new questions, and the liberal democratic tradition has produced some refined approaches to answering them. Canadian courts will undoubtedly need to pay attention to that tradition,

as expressed by Milton, Mill and Anglo-American judicial pronouncements, when it comes to evaluating pornography or hate propaganda legislation in the light of the Charter of Rights and Freedoms.

But it would be foolish for Canadians to rely on the courts alone to determine appropriate limits to coercion and freedom. Courts should not become substitute legislators. The legislation itself should be carried out with a respect for minority rights and freedoms. Otherwise the importance of Parliament with its elected representatives will be diminished as courts have to find acts unconstitutional.

If the courts are to show restraint in striking down legislative acts, the legislature itself will have to act with restraint and awareness of constitutional liberties. Ultimately, the behaviour of the legislators will be affected by the level of awareness of people in their constituency. Hence the recurring need for bringing the complexities of issues like pornography to public attention.

What are the evils that anti-pornography legislation is designed to attack? The most important evil concerns violent sexual crime, which hard-core pornography allegedly promotes. I say "allegedly" because, despite the growing body of social science research establishing a connection between the violent

www.ingramcontent.com/pod-product-compliance
Lightning Source LLC
Chambersburg PA
CBHW081829280526
45789CB00007B/2398